PEOPLE.

HOW TRUE LEADERSHIP AVOIDS EXPENSIVE
MISTAKES, CREATES PROSPERITY, AND
SUSTAINS EXTRAORDINARY BUSINESS

PROCESS.

PROFIT.

PEOPLE.

HOW TRUE LEADERSHIP AVOIDS EXPENSIVE MISTAKES, CREATES PROSPERITY, AND SUSTAINS EXTRAORDINARY BUSINESS

PROCESS.

LORI POLEP, MS

Wall-Street Journal Bestselling Author

PROFIT.

Published by Best Seller Publishing®, St. Augustine, FL
Best Seller Publishing® is a registered trademark.
Printed in the United States of America.
ISBN: 978-1962595179

For more information, please write:
Best Seller Publishing®
1775 US-1 #1070
St. Augustine, FL 32084
or call 1 (626) 765-9750
Visit us online at: www.BestSellerPublishing.org

DEDICATION

To my parents, Anne and Mort Polep, thank you for teaching me so much. Your love and support made me who I am today.

To my children, Jeremy Saffer and Jonathan Polep-Saffer, thank you for all of the joy that you have brought me.

CONTENTS

COMPANY NAMES AND
SIGNIFICANT INFORMATION

1888 — My great-grandfather immigrated to this country from Lithuania.

1898 — My great-grandfather had two farms near Boston, Massachusetts.

1930s — My grandfather went to work for Nemrow Tobacco in Western Massachusetts.

1945 — Mort Polep, my father, started Polep Candy and Tobacco Company.[1]

1961 — Paysaver Catalog Showrooms was started.

1960s–1970s — Creation of Two Annes Leasing and Two Annes Realty Companies. They started using these alternate names also: Polep Brothers Industries and Polep Brothers Distributors. (Unfortunately, I don't know the exact dates.)

1984 — Polep Candy and Tobacco was sold to the Trade Development Corporation.

1986, September — Trade Development Corporation closed due to bankruptcy.

1986, November — J. Polep Distribution Services started business.

1989 — Paysaver Catalog Showrooms closed due to bankruptcy.

2019 — J. Polep Distribution Services was acquired by Palm Beach Capital.

---

[1] My father asked my uncle, Charles Polep, to join him after the company was established.

2020 — Palm Beach Capital formed National Convenience Distribu-
    tors as the umbrella company for the convenience store distrib-
    utors they purchased.

Great-Grandfather Charles Polep and Grandfather Samuel Polep

For more information, please visit

www.LoriPolep.com

INTRODUCTION

(EVERYTHING I KNOW ABOUT BUSINESS I LEARNED AT THE DINNER TABLE)

I come from a long line of businesspeople in wholesale distribution and in retail trade. We have started from scratch in multiple generations. In 1898, my great-grandfather had two farms in the Boston area: Acton and Everett. He also had a wholesale and retail store in Boston in the early 1900s.

My grandfather went to work for a distributor, Nemrow Tobacco, in Springfield after my great-grandfather died. My father worked for Nemrow in high school and then went off to fight in World War II when he was 17. As many young men did in that war, he lied about his age. He was determined to serve.

When this determined young man came out of the army in 1945, he went back to Nemrow Tobacco for a job and asked for a $15 a week raise. When that was refused, my father took his mustering-out pay from the Army — $444 — and started his own business in my grandfather's cellar. It was a candy and tobacco business. He would take orders, bag up the product, and deliver it.[2]

When my grandfather, who worked at Nemrow Tobacco in Springfield, was fired because his son was in competition with them, he came into the business my father started. My uncle joined them

---

[2] My father asked his brother, Charles Polep, to join him in the business at a later date.

with his $444-mustering-out pay. With a $1,000 loan from Shawmut Bank, Polep Candy and Tobacco Company was started.

Over the years, they grew. They acquired other companies and increased the products that they sold. The products were not just ones that were complementary. My father sold TVs, toys, and any product that he could distribute. Eventually, in 1961, he started Paysaver Catalog Showrooms. The catalog showroom industry was an interesting business. Many of the catalog showrooms were started by companies that were in the candy and tobacco business.

I received the foundational knowledge of business at my parents' dinner table. At dinner, I heard discussions of my father buying other companies, acquiring the talent from those companies to join with his company, negotiations with vendors, adding on product lines, and more. Both my parents had an innate understanding of the human side of business, which did not come from a book. They were able to recognize and develop talent within the company. All of this I was lucky to learn by osmosis.

I started in the family business at age eight, counting pennies. I had kept hounding my father to let me go to work with him, so he gave me a job where I could not hurt anything. I was paid in toys. At age ten, on Saturdays during the Christmas season, I was selling toys on the showroom floor. I was definitely the resident expert on toys!

Truly, looking back, I have always felt fortunate that I learned about business so young. I was fortunate I learned the following lessons:

- A strong work ethic will get you further than skills alone
- The importance of completing projects on time and with excellent detail
- The importance of respect
- How to talk to everyone by being a good listener and communicator
- The importance of learning from a fellow employee

- How to describe why one product is better than another
- The importance of not playing pretend
- The importance of cross-selling and organic growth
- How to negotiate with vendors
- How to recognize and develop talent

A STRONG WORK ETHIC WILL GET YOU FURTHER THAN SKILLS ALONE

Being on time, in my family, meant being five minutes early. Not only does it show the person you are meeting, or your employer, that you are dependable and that you have a real interest, but it also allows you the time to get settled and collect your thoughts. I can't tell you how many times I sat in my car waiting, so I wasn't too early, but I had much less stress when I arrived early. This also is true for allowing for travel time.

COMPLETING PROJECTS ON TIME AND WITH EXCELLENT ATTENTION TO DETAIL

Again, being on time shows your interest in the job that you are doing. Providing excellent detail places you above other people doing a similar job in the eyes of your manager. It makes you stand out.

RESPECT FOR OTHERS

How you treat everyone you encounter, whether it is the janitor or the CEO, matters. Their job matters. They matter. You show them this with your body language, good eye contact, a real hello, and listening well, among other things.

HOW TO TALK TO EVERYONE BY BEING A GOOD LISTENER AND COMMUNICATOR

I could easily speak to customers from all walks of life, my fellow co-workers, and management at all levels. This would be important in the future when I became a business and systems analyst.

Although already a good listener, I honed this ability in college as a peer counselor in a drop-in center at Boston University. They gave us a lot of in-depth training. I also took a course in counseling and learned about "active listening." Some of what I learned is below, modified to be relevant here.

Do you listen to hear or listen to respond? If you listen to respond, you will never understand what the person is saying or what their needs are.

What is the customer or business partner looking for? What do we have that would fill their needs?

Are you explaining what you can provide in a way that the customer or business partner understands?

Do you reflect what you hear? (Meaning, do you paraphrase what you heard them say so that you can confirm you're getting it right?)

Do you ask clarifying questions?

Do you listen without judgment?

Show you are interested by nodding your head, looking someone in the eye, and having open body language.

If on the phone, put interest "in" your voice. And do not multi-task, as that can also be heard in your voice.

You can say, "I understand," "Got it," "Uh huh," or something else so that they know you are listening to them.

LEARNING FROM A FELLOW EMPLOYEE

My fellow employees all had more knowledge about their job functions than I, so when I had a question, I learned who to go to who would have the best answers. This will be discussed later in Chapter 5, Activating the Front Line.

Paul Hunziker, my project manager and mentor when I was at IBM, said it like this: "It doesn't matter what you know, it matters that you know who to go to for your answers." (There was no Google then, or even the internet.)

HOW TO TALK ABOUT PRODUCTS

At ten, I could explain why the heavy-duty Tonka truck was so much better than one from another brand, from the heavier metal to the larger, better-quality tires. In my 20s, I did the same with diamonds. Eventually, I did the same with computer systems and with *process improvement*. Except for the toys, whose quality was very apparent to me, I had to learn about the rest. Some knowledge came from people training me, such as in diamonds, and a lot came from research.

DON'T PLAY PRETEND

Don't be afraid to say, "I don't know the answer, but I know where to find more information. Let me get back to you." You will look far more professional than you would giving an incorrect answer.

CROSS-SELLING AND ORGANIC GROWTH

Batteries for the toys, bags for the vacuum cleaner — cross-selling makes your business stronger and more profitable.

Whether you are a distributor stopping at a store, a retail store, someone selling something online, or in some other sales situation, cross-selling makes that sale more profitable. It is much easier to sell more to a current customer than to get a new customer.

Think about McDonald's: "Do you want fries with that?" Or their meal deals.

xviii   Lori Polep

If you have ever bought an inexpensive class or signed up for a webinar online, you might have gotten additional offers such as, "For just an additional X number of dollars, you can get this." When you buy that, another screen comes up with an additional offer. That great $9.99 offer can end up being a lot more, and it might be a great value. This practice is smart selling, as they are selling you more than what was originally offered.

NEGOTIATING WITH VENDORS

My father always said that both sides should leave the table smiling. A vendor can be your best business partner.

RECOGNIZE AND DEVELOP TALENT

I would hear my parents talk about how someone would be good doing a new job; they just had to give them the training. That is where I learned how to recognize and develop talent. Recognizing and developing talent is so important if you want your business to grow. More on that in Chapter 1: Leadership Creation.

LEARNING TO BE AN EXAMPLE

I was always told that, as the owner's daughter, I had to be an example to the employees. I had to work harder and be reliable. I had to treat others with respect.

I had confidence. Hence, two jobs that had a great impact on me were:

1. Complaint Mediator for the Consumer Protection Division for the Attorney General of Massachusetts
2. Systems Analyst/Programmer for IBM Corporate Headquarters

COMPLAINT MEDIATOR FOR THE CONSUMER PROTECTION DIVISION FOR THE ATTORNEY GENERAL OF MASSACHUSETTS

What I learned at the attorney general's office helped me during all my years in business. I found sometimes that I was able to solve complaints against businesses with statements that I'd heard at the dinner table, such as, "When someone is unhappy, they will tell everyone. When you make something right, you have a customer forever."

Two complaints from my work there stand out in my mind. One was that the alternator had stopped working on a Ford that was a month out of warranty. Ford Motor Company intended to make the customer pay for a new one.

I wrote to Lee Iacocca, who was chairman of the board at the time, and said, "I realize that you will not be able to respond to this yourself, but I would appreciate it if you would put me in contact with someone who could."

I explained the situation and said that "The person put their trust in Ford. Now, because of a warranty that was over just a month ago, you will lose a customer because you didn't take care of them. They will remember that."

I received a call from a vice president at Ford who said they would take care of it. The consumer ended up being very happy.

The second one was a contractor who ran over some bushes. The customer was upset and wanted the bushes replaced. I wrote to this contractor, saying, "When someone is unhappy, they will tell everyone. When you make something right, you have a customer forever." That customer was very appreciative also.

It does not take a lot to do something right to make a customer feel like they are well taken care of.

When a customer feels like they matter, they become a loyal customer.

SYSTEMS ANALYST/PROGRAMMER FOR
IBM CORPORATE HEADQUARTERS

When I started at IBM in 1978, we had nine weeks of training to become systems analysts/programmers.

Our instructor told us that 30 percent of the people would fail, and it was up to their manager to decide whether they were able to return to training. The training was split up into three sections. We had to get an 80 or above in each section to stay employed at IBM.

Each of the trainees had three opportunities to fail. However, for at least myself, failure was not an option. Several of us started a study group. It is not an exaggeration to say that I worked harder in those nine weeks than in four years of college. With a thousand applicants for every job there, you can believe that all of us were highly qualified. It was more difficult than I could ever have imagined. The math and computer science trainees had it much easier than the business management trainees, as they already knew a lot of basics, such as the hexadecimal numbering system for reading the information called a "program dump," which was used to figure out where the problem was. I still see the numbers in my mind. My study group and I all made it through.

The training I received there, along with the knowledge I brought with me from growing up in business, helped me to be a stronger, better employee who could solve problems and come up with creative solutions. I would hear my parents talking at the dinner table about something that was happening in the business and how they were going to solve it, so the thought process of how to improve a situation or how to get a better outcome was always present in my mind.

In Chapter 7, Creating Efficiencies for the User Increases Productivity and Profitability, I write about a program that I created for a vice president of IBM, which really shaped how I expected programs to be written. They should be written with the user's productivity and efficiency in mind, and they should be easy to use.

The program I wrote for analysis of the World Wide Database was really my first success at process improvement, although that was not a term I knew at the time.

While at IBM, we were able to join committees. I was always interested in education, so when an opportunity to join the Education Committee came up for our headquarters location, I asked for it. The committee included people from Corporate Headquarters, Data Processing Headquarters, and from two other headquarters locations. We were in charge of creating educational opportunities for new hires.

I remember at one of the meetings, we were talking about how all of the acronyms were very confusing, especially for new hires. I suggested we create an A.L. The chairperson looked at me and said, "What is that?" I said, "An acronym list." We all had a good laugh.

A couple of months later, she called me to her office and offered me the position of Chairperson of the Education Committee, as she was moving to another area of IBM. She said that she could not believe that she was recommending me because she had fought against having me on the committee in the first place, as I was a new hire. She said that my ideas and my work ethic had proved her wrong. She felt that I was the right person for this position. This was an important lesson to me, as I realized that if we don't give someone a chance based on our own beliefs, we could be missing a wonderful asset.

One of the first things I was asked to do was to go to Lexington, Kentucky, with a manager, to review the education program there and compare it to the program in Poughkeepsie, New York, where I had gone for training.

I was then to give a cost-benefit analysis to the director of IT for IBM.

The major difference between the two training programs was that they taught the PL-1 programming language in Lexington versus an IBM internal-use-only programming language in Poughkeepsie.

The key here was that there was so much wasted time and money waiting for the new hires at Corporate Headquarters to be trained in PL-1, as I had needed to be, that it was much more cost-effective to send these new hires out to Kentucky so that they would be able to be productive as soon as they got back from training. The director chose to send the new hires to the program in Lexington.

I also put an event in place for new hires that would give them a good overview of the different areas of IBM. One aspect that other new hires and I found daunting was that we really did not know a lot about the different areas of IBM. Having that information at the beginning would have been helpful. This came into play for me when new people would come into my family business, Polep Brothers Industries, which included Polep Candy and Tobacco Company, Paysaver Catalog Showrooms, Two Annes Realty, and Two Annes Leasing. We would show them around and tell them who people were. It made it much easier for the new hires. We also did this with people who joined us through our acquisitions of other companies. They were able to understand and assimilate into our company.

When I left IBM and started working with Polep Brothers, we were making $78 million in sales, just on the wholesale distribution side. When I first came into the business, I worked with every department to see how the employees performed their functions. For example, I found ways to improve how they entered information. Why have a process take three steps when it could take one? The changes saved time and money.

I was able to bring in technology that helped us increase sales to $200 million in just four years. My father sold the company to the Trade Development Corporation in 1984. We were all still working there. In 1986, TDC went bankrupt. We started over from scratch in November 1986 — and it was at this point that we renamed the company J. Polep Distribution Services. Our first week of sales was $24,000. As of 2019, we were $1.3 billion in sales. What I know is, without a good foundation, we would never have been successful.

Between 1986 and 2019, we added product lines and bought other companies. We expanded from our 60,000-square-foot warehouse (we rented out part of it in the beginning) to 500,000 square feet over five buildings. From 60 employees to over 800, with that total sometimes being over 1,000. We went from servicing Massachusetts, Connecticut, and Rhode Island to all of New England, New York, New Jersey, and Pennsylvania. We had over 100 trucks on the road.

In 1993, we survived what would become known as Marlboro Friday. That was the day Philip Morris cut Marlboro pricing by 20 percent in order to compete with generic cigarettes. Many candy and tobacco distributors who had not diversified into other product lines went out of business. Because we were diversified, we were able to stay in business and get many new customers who needed to find a new distributor. This is why organic growth — referred to also as smart growth — and cross-selling are so important.

THIS BOOK

(A LIFETIME OF EXPERIENCE DISTILLED JUST FOR YOU)

Whether you are creating a new business or want to improve your business, this book provides decades of learning, problem-solving, and strategies for building a business. After a fulfilling career of high-level roles, I started consulting as a strategic advisor for various startups. This line of work has become my passion, and I want to share more of my insights with the world.

From my years learning at the dinner table, through the many successful projects, implementations, training and development, and finding solutions for a multitude of problems, I have organized my experiences into three sections:

1. People
2. Process
3. Profit

In the People section, I talk about the relationships that make your business stronger and build a foundation for growth. Without the people, there is no business, whether it is a customer, employee, or vendor. These relationships, done right, increase your productivity, profitability, and growth.

In the Process section, I talk about several aspects of *process improvement*, which include problem-solving, *continuous improvement*, technology, and Cybersecurity. Inefficient processes can decrease your profitability and can put you out of business.

And finally, the Profit section includes how costs affect your business and how to lower your costs. It includes strategies for growth both within your normal sales channels and expanding into other sales channels, among other ideas.

It has been quite a journey from when my father started Polep Candy and Tobacco Company, plus his other businesses. For some perspective, the business was $78 million in sales in 1980, when I started. It was $200 million in sales when my father sold it to TDC. As I just shared, we started over again in 1986 as J. Polep Distribution Services, with the sales for the first week in business being a little over $24,000. We grew that to over $1.3 billion in sales in 2019, prior to Palm Beach Capital acquiring J. Polep. The company is now National Convenience Distributors, consisting of six family-owned businesses and counting, as they continue acquiring more. These acquisitions and mergers have created a formidable conglomerate comprised of some of the best talent in the Wholesale Convenience Store Distribution business.

I'm excited to share my insights with you. If you're ready to see a world of continuous improvement, let's get to it!

SECTION 1
PEOPLE

"You catch more flies with honey than with vinegar."

— A favorite quote from my mother, Anne Polep

"Both sides should leave the negotiation table smiling."

— A favorite quote from my father, Mort Polep

"People will forget what you said, people will
forget what you did, but people will never
forget how you made them feel."

— Maya Angelou

"Train people well enough so they can leave,
treat them well enough so they don't want to."

— Richard Branson

LEADERSHIP CREATION (POSITIONING FOR GROWTH WITH THE RIGHT PEOPLE IN THE RIGHT PLACE)

To grow a business, you need the right people in the right places.

As shared in my Introduction, J. Polep Distribution Services originally started with my great-grandfather's two farms in 1898. We have started over more than once, and we have evolved into being one of the top five privately held, full-service convenience store suppliers in the United States. Our sales include candy, tobacco, food service, health and beauty care (HBC), and almost any other product you can find in a convenience store. We reached $1.3 billion in sales thanks to the people working here. No business is a great business without its customers and employees.

One thing that is near and dear to my heart is what I call Leadership Creation.

Leadership Creation differs from leadership training and leadership development in that it is not a specific program. It can be used in any size business. It is not expensive, but it is expansive.

Leadership Creation is about recognizing and developing talent. It is working with people who never imagined that they would be leaders. It is about bringing the employee to their discomfort zone but being there for them to mentor them. It is about letting them make mistakes and guiding them through what they learned from those mistakes.

At J. Polep, we have many people who started as customer service reps, receptionists, data entry clerks, pickers in the warehouse, and truck drivers who have grown and developed into managers, directors, and vice presidents of the company.

How do you create these leaders? Truthfully, I learned so much about how to do this by listening to my parents talk about their employees at the dinner table. They talked about how a certain employee should be able to handle more. They would talk about how to give the employee the knowledge and confidence to do the job that had increased difficulty and responsibilities.

We have carried it forward into my generation's running of this business for over 35 years.

MENTORING THROUGH THE PROCESS

A woman who worked for me, Sarah Binney, had been a customer service rep and then came into IT to be a data entry clerk. She was someone who always had a positive attitude. She liked learning new things. She always asked if there was more that she could do. She was self-motivated.

When we were starting a division that provided coffee to offices, we'd purchased new hardware and software to use. We decided that Sarah would be the perfect person to put in charge of this new area.

When I spoke to her about it, she was hesitant. She had no experience running an area. She didn't have enough knowledge. She said that she did not know how to run the software.

I told her, "I will be trained on the software with you. You will be able to ask me questions. I will mentor you through the whole process."

Recently she said that having me and my family believe in her gave her the confidence to go forward. She recalled that I told her that I would rather train someone who doesn't have experience who I can train my way versus someone who just comes in and thinks that they know what they are doing. She also said, "That was one of the things, but just the fact that you believed in me was really important. That you gave me the opportunity and always believed in me. And if I didn't know something, I knew that I could come to you and that you were always there to help me."

Sarah and I did the initial setup of how to run the division. I guided her when she had questions. Running the division was not just about the software, it was about managing all aspects of the division — the customers, the delivery personnel, and the product.

She flew with it! She actually never asked me a lot of questions.

When we decided to sell off the office coffee division, we moved her into sales. She went on to become a district sales manager, then the assistant director of the food service division, and she is now the director of the food service division. The food service division is the fastest-growing part of our business.

All it took was recognizing that she had talent and developing that talent by giving her confidence and opportunities to learn.

There are so many stories like this in the company. As I walked through the offices and warehouse, I saw these people who had worked their way up. I will always be so proud of their accomplishments.

Businesses should always be a place of opportunities for growth for the employees.

By giving people an opportunity to grow, your business has people in place to grow as your business grows. That is key to being able to move on something quickly.

As I said, Sarah moved from running the coffee division into sales. The experience and confidence that she got running that division turned into a great jumping-off point for her. Her experience talking to customers and taking their orders, making sure that the orders got out to the customers, and solving problems as they occurred made her a better salesperson on the road.

As she grew into the other positions, her ability to communicate and her ability to train people when she moved into a management role came from the confidence and interest in learning she had within her. Sometimes all that someone needs is to be given an opportunity and the knowledge to do something out of their comfort zone.

What we gained as a company was someone who was able to move up from a keypunch operator to major positions in the company. To be director of food service at J. Polep is an incredible accomplishment. Sarah does her job really well, as she cares and has acquired knowledge through the years.

I want to mention here that it is important that, as you move someone up, you have someone whom you have been grooming to grow into the position vacated. Ensure that the person who was promoted is willing and able to make time for those who took their old position. This makes growth sustainable.

THE LEADERSHIP CREATION LIST

As you did not have the benefit of dinners with my parents over the decades, I've created my Leadership Creation list.

1. Respect others.
2. Recognize and develop talent.
3. To develop talent, be prepared to teach, but be prepared to listen.
4. No question is stupid.
5. When you teach, if they do not understand it, find other words to explain it.
6. Measure success in displayed understanding.

#1: RESPECT OTHERS

Leadership Creation always starts with respect for others. This is not just for Leadership Creation, it is for all aspects of the company, from the CEO to the janitor. All people are a critical part of the company. All of the employees knew that they could walk into my office, and I would listen.

When people know that you have respect for them, they are more productive. When they know that you listen to them, many will come to you with ideas to improve a process.

I have had situations where something was not working. I would go to the person doing the job to observe and see what was happening. The result is always better, faster solutions. I will talk more about that in the second segment of this book, Process.

#2: RECOGNIZE AND DEVELOP TALENT

It is important to recognize people who are talented, who want to learn, and who want to be challenged. They ask questions and want to learn more. They are self-motivated.

Your critical role as a leader is to recognize that talent — and develop the strengths and confidence of these people. Then you must provide them with new opportunities to grow into new positions within the company and be willing to mentor them. As they grow, other people can grow into their vacated position. It is truly continuous improvement of your employees and, therefore, your company.

Many people have heard about the Peter Principle, where employees are promoted until they become incompetent at their level. I do not think that has to be the case, not with the right mentors and the right training. Some of that training might come from outside the organization. Even a CEO might need some coaching no matter what their background.

I did have someone comment to me once that when someone wants a position or promotion, it is up to them to sink or swim. With that attitude, everyone suffers — the person who failed, their subordinates, their co-workers, and the company. There is a much higher cost associated with someone failing than the cost of getting them training or mentoring them, including demoralizing that person's team, the time and productivity lost by having that person in that position, and the cost of bringing in someone new to take that position, among just a few negative outcomes.

#3: TO DEVELOP TALENT, BE PREPARED TO TEACH, BUT BE PREPARED TO LISTEN

When someone realizes that they can ask questions and have them answered, they will feel free to learn. Making sure that they are comfortable asking you questions is an important step when you are developing the talent and strengths in people.

#4: NO QUESTION IS STUPID

When I first started at IBM's corporate headquarters, Paul Hunziker, my project manager, told me that no question is stupid. He made it easy for me to ask questions and to learn.

I know that some people do not like answering questions more than once. Sometimes to learn a process, people have to hear the answers to their questions more than once.

Have you ever asked a question and thought that you understood that answer only to find that you still had a question? I know that I have. If you are dealing with the type of person who does not like answering questions more than once, they can put you on the defensive. If you do not get the right information, you cannot do your job properly.

I found that with that type of person, it is better to ask for clarification instead of asking the same question. You will need to think about it a bit, but what is it that you do not understand? Asking clarifying questions is much better than asking the same question, as they are then sharing more knowledge with you.

#5: WHEN YOU TEACH, IF THEY DO NOT UNDERSTAND IT, FIND OTHER WORDS TO EXPLAIN IT

I found that when I was teaching or training, there would be times when someone did not understand what I was talking about. I would find another way to tell them or show them.

People have different learning styles, including kinesthetic (touch), auditory, and visual. I found that it was easier for people to learn when two or all styles were combined.

I trained many people on computers. I would be with them, talking them through the process, along with them having a training manual if one had been created. I would have them sit in the seat at the keyboard. We would go through the process as many times as they needed to become comfortable. By having their hands on the keyboard doing the process, such as posting a check to Accounts Receivable and looking at the screen, we had both kinesthetic and visual learning taking place. If I was talking them through the process, they had all three.

There was one person I could not train. It was when I was implementing my first major project at Polep Candy and Tobacco Company (the company's name when I started). The project was to have the salespeople key in their own orders on a handheld mobile unit, thereby skipping the steps of the salespeople calling in their orders to customer service, then the orders being keyed onto a diskette by a keypunch operator, and then taken to the computer for processing.

(For a point of reference, that handheld mobile unit was about the size of a brick and would hold 8,192 bytes (characters) of information, which is 8 kilobytes. A gigabyte is one billion bytes. My iPhone is 256 gigabytes. It amazes me to think about what we were able to do with that little processing power. It would take 32 million units of that handheld to equal my iPhone.)

I sat with the programmers for the handheld unit, our sales manager, and my father to create the program, which included the salesperson being able to key in what money they collected from a customer, so their order could get out faster.

When the program was completed, I asked my father whom I should train first. He told me Don (not his real name). He said that if Don could be trained, then anyone could do it.

I went on the road with Don so that he could have training right at the time of putting in the order. At that time, the salespeople were still writing orders on paper for keypuncher operators to enter in later.

Don could hardly see the keyboard. He was going to be retiring in a year or two. He had no desire to learn something new. After spending a few days on the road trying to train him, I went to my father and said, "Don is having trouble learning this. Give me your best salesperson to train."

I proceeded to train the sales manager and a few of our top salespeople. They learned very quickly. They were excited to learn this because, as I explained it, it gave them more control over their orders. They no longer would have to call in their orders to customer service, who would write them down again, and then they would have to be keypunched in. They went directly to a computer instead. Everything was faster.

After a few salespeople were trained, the two whom I'd trained first started training other salespeople so that we could roll the implementation out faster. This is where I learned what is called today the *Train the Trainer* method. I went on to use it my whole career with the multitude of implementations of hardware and software we had. I would train the managers of the departments and one or two other people of the manager's choosing.

I saw how powerful it was to be trained by people whom you respect and who are doing the same job as you. It is powerful because they understand what your day is like. It puts the power and responsibility in the department with the people doing the job. One key aspect was that people knew they could ask me questions. If I did not know the answer, I would find it. This goes back to No question is stupid.

Don never did learn how to use that unit. But that is okay. He was still a good salesman.

#6: MEASURE SUCCESS IN DISPLAYED UNDERSTANDING

When the people you have trained start offering their own suggestions or using what you've taught them, you know that you have been successful in mentoring them and that they have moved to a new level in their potential.

"WE" VERSUS "YOU"

I really think it is important for you to know that one of the mistakes I made early in my career was using "we" when I shouldn't have. I was talking about how "we" in the department had accomplished something. The system operator felt that I was trying to take credit for something that the programmer/manager did, although my intent had been to say that the department did well. I was very careful after that to make sure I singled out people for the job that they did and left the "we" for a team accomplishment. As a matter of fact, I mostly dropped the "we" and used "you." "We" is very appropriate when "we" are problem-solving and working as a team on a project. Just remember to point it out when someone has achieved a great accomplishment or has made a contribution that should be noticed. People should feel good about what they have accomplished.

In my whole career, there was never a time when I took credit for something I didn't do. Because of that one situation where someone misinterpreted my intent, I became very cognizant of ensuring that people felt recognized. That experience was very educational for me and made me a better leader.

What are your ideas for recognizing and developing talent?

Bring to mind your favorite manager or mentor.

By building a great, sustainable business by creating leaders who grow with the company, you build continuity, engagement, and a happier workforce. Your company is positioned to take advantage of opportunities for growth, which increases your profitability.

KEY TAKEAWAYS

- Recognizing and developing talent makes your company stronger. You build continuity, employee engagement, and a happier workforce.
- Training is critical in increasing an employee's knowledge.
- A good training program decreases your costs and increases productivity.
- By mentoring your employees to help them grow into leadership positions, you position your company to take advantage of opportunities for growth, which increases your profitability.
- Your leaders' and employees' greater efficiency increases profitability.

CHAPTER 2

BUILDING GREAT CUSTOMER RELATIONSHIPS

The facets of great customer relationships are many, but the primary ones are:

1. Trust
2. Respect
3. Products
4. Service

Again, as Maya Angelou said, "People will never forget how you made them feel." Print it out and put it on your computer screens, cash registers, phone, and anywhere else where you interact with customers or anyone else, for that matter. Make it part of your training.

There are many facets to building great customer relationships. The primary one is, How do they feel when they are working with you? Have you evoked a feeling of trust and respect in them? Do they feel that you have their best interest at heart? That is critical for creating a great business relationship. If they don't feel valued, they will buy elsewhere.

I am sure that we all have places that we won't go back to because of how we were treated. Bring that to mind for a minute, and then think of the place you now go to because they treat you well. What do you want people to feel when they buy from you?

LISTENING TO THE NEEDS OF YOUR CUSTOMERS ENHANCES YOUR BUSINESS

Growing up in the business, I learned early on to *listen to hear* what the customer needs. People come to talk to you for your expertise. J. Polep's customers own stores, so they are reselling a product. They want to have a product that will sell, is good quality, and provides a decent profit for them. Whether you are at a clothing store, buying electronics or any other product, or working with a business like J. Polep Distribution Services, a customer wants the same outcome: they want the product to work for them, be of good quality, and be a good value. The customer looks to you for your expertise to make that happen.

Some of our greatest innovations and growth have occurred because of the needs of our customers.

When my father started this business, he sold only candy, cigarettes, and tobacco.

I don't know when he started adding other products, but when I started there full-time, there were two main businesses. One was the wholesale candy and tobacco business, with candy, cigarettes, tobacco, sundries, and health and beauty care (HBC). The other was our retail catalog showroom business, which carried jewelry, photo equipment, luggage, small appliances, and many other products. Very similar to a Kohl's without the clothes.

Adding products is key to having a successful business.

PRODUCT LINES BASED UPON TRENDS AND NEW PRODUCTS (PROVIDING INCREASED SALES AND PROFITABILITY TO YOU AND YOUR CUSTOMERS)

When a customer comes into your store or when you are making a delivery, it is so much more profitable to sell multiple products to them. A company that is famous for that is McDonald's: "Do you want fries with that?" Or the meal combos. You might be getting a good deal, but they are making more profit because they are selling you three products versus one. More about this will be covered in Chapter 13 (Smart and Organic Growth).

The key to this is selling products that the customers want and that they feel can increase their profits. One of the first major product lines that we added was groceries. This made us attractive to the convenience store chain Dairy Mart, which had 200 stores. Of course, once you get one major chain, it is easier to get others when you build a great reputation for service and products.

Choosing products that will do well for a customer is key to successful business growth.

When a customer sees that the product you recommended did well for them, you build trust. When you recommend something else, they are more open to buying it. Over time, a synergistic relationship is built, where your company and your customer are business partners.

Over the years, we have added many different product lines. Sometimes I wonder which came first, the growing needs of convenience stores, or did we create an awareness of what items a convenience store could add to make them more profitable? I think that it is a combination.

First, it is being aware of what the marketplace is doing. How is it changing? What is available now? What are the new trends? To discover that information, you might attend trade shows and conventions. We have always gone to conventions and tradeshows. Their look and their scope have changed through the years. My parents would always go to the candy convention for the wholesale business and the jewelry show for the retail business. They also attended other trade shows. Trade shows and conventions are where we find out what is new and innovative in the market.

We also look at trade publications and at what our competitors are doing. Often, we will hear from our customers or our salespeople about what a competitor is offering.

We sometimes have vendors come to us with products and new technologies. This is also a key element to building a strong business. I will be discussing that in more detail in Chapter 3, Your Vendors as Partners.

I do believe that having good relationships with customers helps you grow and helps you keep your business operating well. Years ago, our departments contributed representatives to a focus group that would go to different customers and talk to them about what we were doing well, what we could do better, and what they saw for future growth for their company. This group consisted of IT, Sales Administration, and management from the sales team. This helped us be proactive. We could look at the technical solutions and the products as well as the food and product programs the customers needed for growth. There were many times that the customers were not aware that we offered something, whether it was a technical solution or a product we had that would be able to fill their needs.

Today, a well-designed company website can be very beneficial because it can showcase a company's products, history, values, technology, and more. It can create a desire to do business with someone, whereas a poorly designed website can push people away.

I remember in 2002 or earlier, I learned FrontPage and HTML. It is always important to know HTML, even today, as websites often need tweaking behind the scenes, and sometimes you want the ability to make a change immediately, without waiting for your website designer. Of course, back then, there weren't many web design companies. We decided to create our own website.

I created a cross-functional team to get the information for the website. We created About Us, Technology, Locations, Events, Products, and New and Featured Products pages so that we could keep the customers informed. At that time, not everyone saw the need for a website, but shortly after it went live, the VP of new accounts and the VP of chain accounts went to see a potential customer. This prospect's team had all of the web pages printed and spread out in front of them. Having the story relayed at a management meeting really solidified the need for and the power of a website. The website has grown and changed over the years. Today, a social media presence is also mandatory for business.

THE MESSAGE
(MAKING YOUR CUSTOMER AWARE OF WHAT IS AVAILABLE AND HOW IT CAN HELP THEIR BUSINESS)

Whatever you are selling, whether it is products for a convenience store, Lasik eye surgery, law services, and so on, you must get the message across of what you are selling and its benefits to your customer. For doctors, lawyers, and other types of services, that will be via the internet, ads on TV and radio, and even billboards. For us, the best way for our customers to learn about what we have and what is new are our company's trade shows, where the customer can see and try many of the products. The customer can see how a coffee machine, a slushy machine, and other machines work.

For the J. Polep trade shows, the buyers work hard with vendors to set up deals with great pricing for our customers. Our customers (retailers) arrive looking for new products and those deals. They look at the food service programs that are available to them, and quite often, the deals come with enough product to offset the cost of the machine. They are thrilled to get the opportunity to grow their business with the products presented to them. A major benefit is that they are taking one day off from their stores and seeing the most current products, equipment, and ideas all under one roof.

Even vendors like M&M Mars put together deals that make the retailer very profitable.

This is a win-win-win situation. The vendor has sold a lot of products, the retailer will make a larger profit, and J. Polep, as the wholesaler, has also sold more products. The customer has new ideas as to how to improve their sales with new products, new food service programs, and new technology.

When you walk into a convenience store today, you might see pizza, ice cream, a deli, a roller grill for hot dogs, breakfast items, and so on. You will always see coffee, but that was not always true. We have helped retailers develop their own fresh sandwich programs, so when you walk into a store serviced by J. Polep, you are able to get great sandwiches, salads, and even yogurt parfaits. That all came from innovation among the wholesaler, the vendor, and the retailer. This is all part of cross-selling. When you can offer products that the customer entering the store wants, you are making the whole supply chain more profitable.

What about your company? No matter what you sell, it is about how you can help the customer. You create a much more profitable business by recognizing customers' needs. By cross-selling to them. By creating profitability for customers who are resellers. By having service channels that support the customer. If you are in technology, how will your solution help the customer? What support do you supply that will help them get the result that they need? If you want additional sales and good referrals, you need the customer to feel valued. Many companies sell the same or similar products and services. *What makes you stand apart?*

KEY TAKEAWAYS

- Listening to your customers' needs helps you create a better company.

- Creating increased profitability for your customers via cross-selling and offering them programs to help build their business builds your business and increases your profits.
- Building a relationship of trust makes it easier for you to expand your business with your customer.

CHAPTER 3

YOUR VENDORS AS PARTNERS

Without our phone system, we could not do business.

Replacing a phone system with 200 lines and, additionally, 200 voicemail-only lines was a huge undertaking.

Acada Communications was introduced to us by Amy Gerber at Tel-Affinity.

We all became part of a team to get this project in and running successfully.

Although I am mostly going to speak about Acada Communications here, Amy handled the vendors bringing the lines into the system. When we would have an issue, her response was not just to call this number, she would follow through with the companies also.

Brian English and his team at Acada were not only responsive, they were also proactive.

They would call us about planning a system upgrade if they saw something that was a concern to them, even if we did not see it.

Great vendor relationships like these increase profitability, decrease costs, and increase sales. They are partnerships versus just being a sales channel for a quick buck.

I dealt with a vendor once who had a great price on corrugated boxes. Now, boxes might not be something that your customers would understand the importance of. We bought boxes by the trailer load — at least a couple of loads a month of 20,000 boxes of one type and 16,500 of another. The boxes had to be manufactured for us in certain sizes, and they had to be able to hold a certain weight so that when they were loaded onto a truck, we could have several boxes on top of each other.

I always asked for samples and ran a test to see if this vendor's boxes would work for us. That went fine. A year later, our warehouse supervisor came to me and said that the boxes were being crushed. That meant that when a box would get crushed at the bottom of the pile, all the boxes would fall, and there would be damaged products. Damaged goods meant the following:

Our customer would not get the product. They would get a credit, but they would not have the product to sell.

We had to absorb the cost of damaged products.

We had to absorb the cost of redelivering the products.

The damaged products would have to be rekeyed to create another order.

Definitely a huge cost.

I had kept the original box that this vendor gave me as a sample. I could see that they made the subsequent boxes lighter. I quickly found another box vendor, Mount Tom Box,[3] who did a fabulous job for us. We never had to worry about boxes again, as they were a company that made a great product and were honest. Additionally, their salesperson was always there to answer any of my questions.

There are a few vendors who are on my "Do not ever do business with again" list. Fortunately, they are few and far between.

BUILDING A RELIABLE SALES CHANNEL BUILDS TRUST

What makes a business great to work with is that they are reliable and they have great products or solutions for your customers that are delivered on time.

---

[3] Mount Tom Box is now part of Key Container Corporation.

This means that everything that flows into your business — how an order is processed, how it is delivered, and more — must work well together. One of the worst nightmares a business can have is when a vendor does not deliver products on time or is not delivering services properly.

Let us be frank here. The customer does not want to hear about why you could not deliver the product. They have a business to run. Their business depends upon your ability to deliver the products and services that they need. Customers have options as to where to buy their products and most services. If you have issues often, they will find someone else.

How often have you been concerned that products you've ordered might not come in on time? How will that affect you? A product not delivered to us, as distributors, could mean that hundreds of customers do not get the product that they need. How you are affected as a business is multiplied by how many of your customers are affected.

There are so many potential breakpoints in the process of servicing your customers. You want to choose vendors who help make you more profitable, as they offer great products and they are willing to help you sell the products. The vendors who are offering services can help make you more efficient and reduce your costs. The wrong vendor can erode or even destroy what you have built.

In business, it is great to work with people who make it easier for you to do business together.

We have many incredible vendor relationships.

For instance, there is one broker, Harold W. Young Partners (HWY), that we have been doing business with for decades — back to my grandfather's time. I remember meeting Harold's son Jerry, who was my father's generation, when I started in the business full-time in 1980. My father had a way of introducing someone whom he valued and trusted, although I really cannot describe it.

It was the smile on my father's face and the tone of his voice that conveyed the trust.

Today, we continually work together to bring products to market. When HWY brings us an item, they have already vetted it and the company that is producing it. HWY has grown tremendously along with us, because while they helped us build our business with great products and service, we have helped them grow by giving them a sales channel that they can depend upon. Not only have they grown with us through the years but the business relationship is generational. We have worked extensively with Jerry's son, Andy Young, who is co-president with his sister, Betsy Harris,[4] and BJ Gomeau, VP of convenience, in the same way that my father and grandfather did, in a relationship built on trust.

THE VALUE OF BUILDING STRATEGIC VENDOR RELATIONSHIPS

Building connections and relationships with vendors will help your company:

- Increase profit margins through strategic planning
- Boost customer loyalty, reputation, and word of mouth
- Improve the quality of your company's products or services
- Decrease operating costs through streamlined processes and reduced inventory
- Choose the best technology to grow and support your business
- Reduce your time dealing with problems as they take ownership of issues and work with you to solve problems

A good relationship with a vendor will increase their sales and profitability too.

---

[4] Andy leads the convenience team, and Betsy leads the grocery team.

As a distribution business, we always looked for the best products and deals to bring to our customers. Even the vendors of products that we carry that have no competition, such as M&M Mars, want to introduce new products and increase sales of their product lines.

We give all of the vendors that we deal with the opportunity to do that.

The vendors we've dealt with have always known that they could bring a product to us, and if we thought that it would work for our customers, we would work to promote it. In return, they would provide sales contests or promotional monies to get the product introduced to our customers. In many cases, we were able to get them to agree to give credit for a product if it did not sell.

It was standard for us to ask, "What introductory deal will the customer receive?" Most vendors would offer that up front, as they were aware of what was needed for a customer to try a new product.

That is one of the keys to working with a vendor. Know what you want for the outcome and have the vendor know that these are the parameters.

By being able to bring new products to your customers, you help their sales increase. A good vendor will promote a product to you that will increase your customers' sales, which has the domino effect of increasing the sales of everyone involved.

IMPORTANT VENDOR SERVICES/SOLUTIONS

When you add a sale of a product to a delivery, by nature, you increase the profitability of that delivery. This is true for every company, whether you are adding products to a service provided or creating a combination of products (as in, adding fries to your meal). We'll talk more about this in Chapter 13 (Smart and Organic Growth).

We depend on our vendors to bring these new items to us. We also depend on them to solve certain problems, depending on the type of vendor.

The vendors we want to work with are those we can rely on to:

1. Bring us high-quality products so that we can expand our product lines to our customers
2. Deliver product on time and in good condition
3. Solve issues with the products they sell to us
4. Work with us when a product isn't selling
5. Provide support to our salespeople, which could be product information and samples
6. Provide sales incentives and deals

BRING US HIGH-QUALITY PRODUCTS SO WE CAN EXPAND OUR PRODUCT LINES TO OUR CUSTOMERS

With our goal to provide products that add to our customers' bottom line, we have looked for product lines and add products within those lines that consumers would be interested in buying.

For example, in the late '90s, convenience stores recognized that offering a better cup of coffee would attract people to their stores. We tested several coffee brands and decided on Baronet Coffee, owned by the Goldsmith family. Bruce Goldsmith was the type of vendor we were looking for. He had a great product, great support, and worked hard to help us to grow.

When someone wants a cup of coffee today, they have many options, such as dark roast, medium roast, different blends, and flavored. Customers' expectations have increased, and the ability to offer options is critical as someone will choose to go to the store down the road to get the coffee they desire.

Bruce has expanded several times. I met with him in his newest building as I was editing this book. I commented that his building is impressive. He said, "It is because of you." ("You" meaning J. Polep.) Actually, we grew together. Baronet's growth is a testament to how Bruce strives for excellence in his products and his service to his customers, and it's an example of how great partnerships create success for both companies.

Another example of adding products to meet the changing customers' needs is when natural and organic products started to become popular. We increased our product lines to include those. Additionally, companies like KIND and Clif Bar kept on expanding their lines as consumers changed their habits, such as expanding into protein bars and eventually gluten-free bars. Clif Bar made the LUNA Bar for women's needs in 1999, and in 2003 committed to using only organic ingredients where available.[5] Recently, I bought a Lola Bar, which is a prebiotic and probiotic bar. These types of innovations have created a line of products, driven by customers who want healthy, easy nutrition on the go. The evolution of the bar and other healthy options is remarkable.

DELIVER PRODUCT ON TIME AND IN GOOD CONDITION

When products are not delivered on time or are not in good condition, we can't sell them to our customers. As I said before, we have to be able to service our customers. They will not care that the delivery truck with a truckload of Hershey product broke down and that all the chocolate is melted. Our customers want their product. The vendor needs to make it right very quickly by getting us enough to get through the next few days until they can get another truckload out to us. In rare instances, we have bought pallets of product from Costco, just to have enough of the top sellers to ship when a vendor has had an issue. But that is definitely a Band-Aid, not the full solution.

---

[5] Karin Kinkaid Thrift, Director of Sales/Convenience Store Channel

We are fortunate to have secondary suppliers also. That helps in a situation like this or if a vendor just doesn't have enough product.

If it is a food item, it must have an expiration or sell-by date that is reasonable. As distributors, we commit to our customers that they will have a reasonable amount of time to sell the product before the expiration date on the package. That is why it is important that a product's date is checked upon receipt in our warehouse and that the information about that product is captured in the computer system. It also is important for returns, as we can tell when an item was last purchased. If it was purchased long before the expiration date, we can surmise that the stock wasn't rotated properly on the customer's shelf and that they were not entitled to a credit.

We use licenses that follow the product through the warehouse that have all of the information needed about that product, including lot number in case of recalls.

We also know which items have been delivered first so that we can get that product out first.

SOLVE ISSUES WITH THE PRODUCTS THEY SELL TO US

Sometimes an order comes in where some or all of the products in the order are damaged. The vendor has to come in and make it right by giving us a credit and quickly replacing what was damaged. If it was a minor loss, we will be flexible and wait for the next order. If the loss affects our ability to have product for our customers, they really need to jump to make this right.

WORK WITH US WHEN A PRODUCT ISN'T SELLING

There will always be a time when a product won't sell. Will the vendor help you move it by finding another distributor where the product is selling, or will they set up a special deal so that the customers will buy it at a lower price?

PROVIDE SUPPORT TO OUR SALESPEOPLE, WHICH COULD BE PRODUCT INFORMATION AND SAMPLES

Some representatives will ride along with a salesperson to introduce a product.

It is easier to sell an item if the salesperson has tried it and has some samples to show their customers. Also, a ride-along with a representative from the vendor helps the company promote the product as that person is more knowledgeable about the product than our salesperson, who sells 12,000 items. Customers always like to meet someone from the vendor who is representing the product.

PROVIDE SALES INCENTIVES AND DEALS

It helps to sell a product when a vendor provides sales incentives, which could be money for each item or deal sold, tickets to a baseball game for the highest producer, a trip for the highest producer, gift cards, and so on.

Deals are important as a customer will be able to introduce the product at a better price. Deals also are important to promote more sales. Buy two candy bars for just a little more than buying one will increase sales. (Who doesn't want a deal?)

TYPES OF VENDORS

Your company might have other ways for a vendor to partner with you.

There are several types of vendors:

1. Resale
2. Production
3. Service Providers

THERE ARE VENDORS FOR ITEMS THAT ARE RESOLD

As a distributor to convenience stores, items that we carry are resold to our retailers. Whether it is coffee, M&M's, or pizza crust, these items go to retailers to be sold or used in production.

THERE ARE VENDORS FOR PRODUCTION

I wrote earlier about corrugated boxes. Think about a pizza shop that was out of pizza boxes. That is a critical part of their production. I remember going to a pizza shop and being told that they were only selling small pizzas, as they'd run out of large boxes. They told me that their order did not come in. WOW!

Many items are needed for production. For our distribution company, this includes shrink wrap, corrugated boxes, labels, forms, printers, and ink, just to name a few.

The question for you is, what production items would stop you from doing business if you were out of them? What is that cost versus having more on hand? More about that in the Process section.

THERE ARE VENDORS WHO PROVIDE SERVICES

We need many vendors to stay operational. The conveyors have to run. The trucks have to be on the road, not in the repair shop. We have an extensive computer network. We have multiple ways to receive orders and a robust phone system.

Every company needs a phone system. What is the cost of lost orders if the pizza shop lost its phone system for the day? Or its electricity? Or the pizza oven? What if it happens more than once? What happens to the credibility of that pizza shop? People will go elsewhere quickly.

This is why it is critical to have great service providers, as they:

- Provide solutions that work for your business

- Resolve issues that occur
- Work with companies that take responsibility for a system, versus finger-point and say it's not their problem

AN INCREASING RELATIONSHIP

Working with dependable vendors increases your company's reliability — you have less downtime.

You increase profitability, as the more efficiently you can run your business, the easier it is to grow. Working with vendors who offer you great deals to pass on to your customers, and who do ride-alongs with salespeople so that a new product can be introduced to a retailer, help the profitability of the company. Vendors are an integral part of the team, so when you have an issue or a question, reach out to them to help rectify it. You get faster results by communicating issues. Also, communicate to them what they are doing right, as a good partnership goes both ways.

Great vendor relationships increase profitability, decrease costs, and increase sales. Find the vendors who are partners in your growth, and replace those who aren't, as quickly as possible.

KEY TAKEAWAYS

- Look for vendors who want to see you succeed through product support, deals, credits, follow-through, and on-time delivery.
- Find an alternative source if a vendor is giving you substandard service or product.
- A reliable sales channel builds trust and profitability whether it be for products or services.
- A great sales partner will target new products to increase sales and profits for you and your customers.

- Being on the cutting edge of technology will provide better delivery times and better customer service. It will also give you and your customers tools for analysis — which in turn enables you to improve and sustain a better quality of service.
- The better your service, the more secure your profitability will remain!

SECTION 2
PROCESS

"If hindsight were foresight, we would be a far sight better."

— Another of my mother, Anne Polep's,
favorite quotes. This is why we have preventative
maintenance and continuous improvement, among
other things, as hindsight can be costly.

CHAPTER 4

PROCESS IMPROVEMENT = GROWTH AND PROFITABILITY

"We shall not cease from exploration
And the end of all our exploring
Will be to arrive where we started
And know the place for the first time."

—T. S. Eliot

I was in college when I first saw this quote by T. S. Eliot. It became a constant in all aspects of my learning, whether college, IBM, business, or just life itself. Those AHA moments lead to understanding and then growth.

Process Improvement is that. It starts with where we are, exploring how to make something better, and seeing what steps we need to take to improve where we are. Process improvement moves a company from *just being* to *being the best*.

Often, process improvement happens when we see a problem that has to be fixed. Sometimes having to resolve an issue under pressure ends up being a Band-Aid, and the same or a similar problem occurs. You were able to become operational again — there will always be situations that require a quick response and resolution. The key is to revisit that problem to see if a process needs to be changed so that it won't happen again. Correcting a problem is what makes you more profitable.

It is much more costly to correct a problem when it is an emergency than to improve upon the process and reduce or eliminate the issue. We had five miles of conveyors throughout our buildings. When something went wrong, it would stop our whole picking process. Deliveries would be late. A delay in deliveries might cost tens of thousands of dollars in overtime and rekeying orders — when the fix was a $2 dollar part. The warehouse started keeping certain parts on hand but, much more importantly, they entered into a preventative maintenance program.

Preventative maintenance is probably one of the most straightforward solutions to see and implement. There are other aspects of process improvement that are critical to growth and profitability, such as Continuous Improvement and Business Process Review.

Continuous improvement keeps your company on top of the more minor, incremental changes that allow your company to stop issues before they become significant problems, creating more efficient business processes. Continuous improvement happens best when there are cross-functional teams that can work on streamlining business processes and creating a better workflow. The teams keep communication open between different areas of the company, creating better solutions.

Business process review (BPR) is critical — for example, when looking for new computer software such as a new ERP (Enterprise Resource Planning) package that runs all aspects of a company. It includes order processing, financials, delivery, warehousing, and much more. It is critical to review what you have in place now. If you don't clearly understand what your current software is doing, it is easy to make an error when choosing new software. Some of your company's processes that make your business efficient might not be available in the new software. What will it cost to customize the software? Why are you moving to new software?

I find that a gap analysis is helpful when conducting a BPR. It will show you where you are while identifying where you want to be. In between where you are and where you want to be is the cost of modifications needed. There are software tools available that will go in depth asking questions and defining what your current processes are. This document, called a Request for Proposal — or RFP — is filled out by people in their departments and reviewed as a cross-functional team. This completed RFP would be sent to the companies whose software you want to see. They answer the RFP in depth. You would then review the companies with a cross-functional team to see if they are a fit. The cross-functional team is critical, as you might have to change processes to make the software work for you without modifications.

Some questions to ask your team are:

- What can your company live without?
- How does the software improve your company?
- How do we do business without certain functionality, or are modifications needed?
- Is this company capable of making your needed modifications?

The above is a simplified version of a long process.

Armed with this information, you will get pricing from the vendor. This process might lead to you deciding that your current system is the best fit and might just require a rewrite of some of your existing software. Or it might lead you to buying new software. Either way, you have a much deeper understanding of your business processes and requirements.

There are so many powerful tools to help with process improvement. I have used many through the years. Mostly, any identifiable problem can be solved through these tools and improved by changing processes. Process improvement is key to a well-run company. The first step is to understand and define the problem using a tool like Root Cause Analysis.

ROOT CAUSE ANALYSIS

I have used Root Cause Analysis often, using the **5 Whys methodology,** which can be more than five questions. Often, the problem that you are seeing is not the cause of the problem. Fixing only what you see means that you will have this problem again as you didn't get to the actual cause. For example, a conveyor breaks, causing four hours of a delay in picking an order. Here is how the 5 Whys could be used, and it is often more than five whys:

Orders will be delayed by four hours.
Why will they be delayed?
The conveyor broke.
Why did the conveyor break?
One of the rollers came loose.
Why is it going to take so long to fix it?
The repair company has to get the part.
Why don't we have the part here?
We handle problems as they come up.
Why aren't we on a preventative maintenance program?
It was expensive.

How high is the cost of being down for you? That instance was probably a cost of over $40,000 in overtime to get the orders out and delivered, plus the cost of customers being upset that their order was late. Customer dissatisfaction is why you lose customers.

OBSERVATION

Another tool that I use extensively is Observation. In real estate, the three most important factors are Location, Location, Location. In process improvement and problem determination, they're Observation, Observation, Observation. In observation, I include listening. Listening to hear the problem, not to respond. When you listen to respond, you don't hear all of the information; therefore, you cannot understand the problem. Get all of the information first.

Later, in Chapter 5: Activating the Front Line, you will see why observation is so important and why working with the people who are doing the actual job will give you the best solution.

Observation is also important in other areas. When hearing that someone is having an issue with something or improvement is needed, I will talk to them and see what they are doing. Their task might require a simple modification to give them the best solution.

Process improvement is essential. What is even more important is prevention. Ben Franklin said, "An ounce of prevention is worth a pound of cure." Prevention is what comes from good planning.

When you have a car, it needs maintenance done on a timely basis. You plan for that. If you skip it, your car could need significant work in the future, or you could break down at the worst possible time.

How about being able to avoid problems before they happen?

CONTINUOUS PROCESS IMPROVEMENT

Continuous process improvement means continually evaluating what you are doing and making small, incremental changes. Several aspects of it are:

Lean methodology: The primary precept of Lean is to maximize customer value while minimizing waste.

Kaizen: This is part of Lean strategy where employees at all levels and multiple departments of a company work together to achieve continual, incremental improvements.

Continuous learning: Educating your employees and yourself is critical to running your business efficiently and growing your business.

What-If analysis/Risk analysis: Let's say you have a large project and it is based upon several things working together. Performing a What-If analysis based upon each segment of the project will help you determine possible issues. Identifying these issues in the planning stage decreases risk and increases the outcome of a successful project. Including the departments affected by or benefiting from this project allows for problem determination before a problem occurs.

Cross-functional teams: When a project or a problem affects multiple departments, it is critical to create a cross-functional team because the members will talk about how they are affected and will have input on their needs. You are creating a solution for the whole company, not just one department.

Six Sigma: [6] Six Sigma methodology has become the standard for process improvement.

It is based on five principles:

1. Identifying Root Causes of Problems
2. Maximizing Customer Value
3. Continuous Process Improvement
4. Collaboration and Coordination with Teams and Management
5. Agility and Versatility

Using the Six Sigma methodology increases productivity and efficiency tremendously. Six Sigma provides a road map companies can use to plan for growth and to create solutions for problems. There are several levels of training available that are worth exploring.

KEY TAKEAWAYS

- When a problem needs to be solved quickly so that you are operational, review what happened to see if a process needs to be changed so that you don't repeat the problem. Repeatedly Band-Aid-ing an issue is costly.

---

[6] "The Six Sigma Process Explained and Tips to Start Implementing It Today," *Simplilearn Solutions*, last updated on Nov 22, 2021.

- Cross-functional teams build a better solution. A problem in one area of the company affects many areas. Streamlining a process helps many areas of the company and increases profitability by creating efficiencies.
- Continuous improvement is the backbone of a strong, profitable company. It allows for efficient, small changes over time versus a major overhaul.
- Using the tools named in this chapter will help you resolve problems and find solutions more quickly. Using continuous process improvement can help you avoid many problems. You will improve your business, decrease costs, increase productivity and profitability, and have improved customer and employee satisfaction.

5

ACTIVATING THE FRONT LINE: PROBLEM-SOLVING AT THE SOURCE

What would you do if you were in management meetings hearing about problems that people are having no luck solving? Would you just say that it is someone else's problem, as it is not your department? Or would you think that this problem, which affects the profitability and efficiency of the company, is your problem also?

I was faced with that when we had spent $2 million retooling the whole warehouse to be more efficient, adding miles of conveyors, an automated system for scanning the bundles onto trucks, and placement of product so that the faster-moving products were in the middle shelves for picking. Think of a bay, four shelves high and with five pick slots for each shelf. You can walk through a grocery store or convenience store, look at the shelves and the aisles, and imagine what it would be like to be moving quickly through a warehouse, picking, labeling, and packing hundreds of items in just one order.

Instead of the pick, pack, and load process becoming more efficient, we had a 27 percent error rate when we flipped the switch to the new system. Picking was so slow that even executives were coming in to pick orders at night. Wrong items were being picked. Trucks were getting out late. Customers were getting upset.

I listened to this for three weeks. No one could understand why we were having the problems that were costing us at least $1 million in miss-picks a week. That was over and above the increased costs of overtime and late trucks. My thought process was that we must solve this problem before it puts us out of business and before we start losing customers.

R.O.L.E. FOR PROBLEM RESOLUTION

I initiated what I call my 4-part process (R.O.L.E.) for solving problems, which evolved from troubleshooting many situations throughout the years.

1. **R**ecognize
2. **O**bserve
3. **L**isten
4. **E**xplore

One: ***R****ecognize and acknowledge that there is a problem or an opportunity for improvement.*

The only way a problem can be solved, or a process can be made more efficient, is to recognize the need for improvement.

Two: ***O****bserve where and how the work is being done.*

If you don't see how the work is being done, you will have no idea how it can be improved.

Three: ***L****isten to the people doing the work.*

The people doing the work will provide insight into why the problem is occurring. From this, you will have the information to create a solution that will solve the problem.

Four: ***E****xplore possible solutions with them.*

When a solution is agreed upon, they own the solution.

EXPLORING POSSIBLE SOLUTIONS

Questions you should always ask when looking for the source of a problem are:

1. Is it training?
2. Is it software?
3. Is it hardware?
4. Is it a combination of some or all of the above?

#1: IS IT TRAINING?

Unless you know that it is a mechanical, hardware, or software issue, I suggest looking at training first. Training is very often the culprit, as jobs change and people doing the jobs change.

When the people who initially did the job leave or get moved to another position, they often don't pass on all of what they know because they don't realize that it is important.

It is also human nature to forget, so it is essential to have a good, updated training manual and how-to videos where applicable.

#2: IS IT SOFTWARE?

Does the software need an upgrade? Have you outgrown its capabilities? Software always needs upgrades. Sometimes they are not performed on a timely basis, or sometimes you have outgrown the capabilities of the software.

If you have a smartphone, think back to your first one. What did it do? What can it do today?

#3: IS IT HARDWARE?

Just as with software, hardware also needs upgrades or replacement. Often, when you upgrade software, you will need to upgrade or replace the hardware too. Again, think of the capabilities of mobile phones when they first came out versus smartphones today. Also, as software grows and becomes more complex, more robust hardware is needed to run that software.

#4: IS IT A COMBINATION OF SOME OR ALL OF THE ABOVE?

What is important to note is the hardware and software become obsolete. The need for training and process improvement is constant.

So, given the above, how do you resolve this issue as quickly and in the best way possible?

THE BEST, QUICKEST RESOLUTION

It is important to observe how a job is being accomplished. You will learn more by observing and asking questions than by trying to resolve this from an office.

In the instance with the high error rate of the new picking system, I went to see how the order selectors were being trained.

The trainer, Russ Kemp, was excellent. I listened to how he was training the order selectors. I heard several issues, the biggest being that the VP of Warehouse Operations, Scott (not his real name), had changed the numbering system of the shelf labels.

Going up the right-side aisle next to the conveyer, Scott had the pick slots labeled from the lowest number to the highest.

Going down the left-side aisle next to the conveyer, Scott changed it to be the highest number from the right going down from the highest to the lowest number.

So, the right-side read "Bay 1, shelf 1, slot 1" — whereas the left side read "Bay 25, shelf 1, and slot 4" (even though it was really the first slot on that side). You might ask, Why does this matter?

Changing the numbering of pick slots from one side to the other is very disorienting. The brain doesn't work that way, as it is not logical. Add on the high rate of speed that the order is picked at, and it is a recipe for disaster.

I called over Joe Randazzo, the warehouse supervisor, and pointed out the issue. He said that he had told Scott that it would not work. Scott didn't listen to him. Joe thanked me when I said that we would have the labels changed back immediately.

We went to the programmer to ask how long it would take to print the labels in the right order. He was able to do it within a day. Joe got people in the warehouse to work over the weekend to relabel the slots. Once the slots were relabeled, the miss-picks dropped to 7 percent — still high, but we also fixed other problems that I saw while observing the training.

They all had to do with labeling on the shelf.

One problem was that high-velocity items could have several facings on the shelf. The warehouse worker would put the label in the middle of the shelf. Their trainer was training the workers to look to the right and left of the shelf label to see if there were multiple slots. I was told that this was a big problem, as order selectors were missing the items mainly to the right of the slot label.

Again, speed and the inconsistency of the shelf labeling process were a problem. If an order selector was moving quickly from left to right and saw an empty slot where the product was supposed to be, they usually would not look to the right as they were moving left. They would mark the item as not available. However, the system would still show that the product was in the slot, as the one label was really for the amount in the five slots. Some errors would be found by someone checking the order, but not enough.

Looking at this, I asked Russ, "What if we create an overflow label, as in, we put the shelf label on the rightmost slot and have an overflow label pointing to each of the overflow slots, until the next item is reached?" He loved the idea. We made those fluorescent green.

The other issue was that there were items in the single pick area where packages had to be opened, so you weren't picking a package of six toothbrushes when it should be one toothbrush that was picked.

That is fine, as long as that was true for all items. But there were some items whose whole package needed to be kept intact, such as the Lil' Drug Store items. As I heard the trainer tell the trainees that this item should not be opened, my thought process was "With the thousands of items in the warehouse, there is no way anyone can remember which items should not be opened." I came up with the idea of putting a large "Do Not Open" label next to the shelf label. When I spoke to the trainer about it, he said that would work. We made those labels fluorescent orange.

During this process, Joe told me they also had a problem with putting away the product. If someone stocks a product facing the wrong direction, they run out of space on the shelf. He came up with a label with an arrow that he put on the back of a gravity feed shelf or on the front of a static shelf that shows the person stocking the shelf the direction that the case should be placed. The labels were round green dots with an arrow.

When this was implemented, we dropped our error rate to 3 percent, which was acceptable.

Did you notice that I mentioned the colors of the labels? Colors are important. Once people were used to the picking process, all they needed to see was the color in order to know what to do.

This impossible problem was solved in a few hours of observing and listening. It is critical that the people doing the job are asked for input and listened to. Had the warehouse supervisor been listened to, millions of dollars would have been saved.

Observing the training allowed me to see what issues there were. Bringing the warehouse supervisor into the discussion gave me a greater understanding of the problem. It allowed us to come up with workable, inexpensive solutions. The biggest expense came from not listening.

We can't solve problems with a top-down approach; they are solved when we Activate the Front Line.

KEY TAKEAWAYS

The R.O.L.E. process works in multiple situations. Listen to those doing the job when you are in the planning phase. A key factor in this incredibly expensive mistake was not listening to Joe, who knew that changing the numbering system was not logical and would fail. Let's use R.O.L.E. on the story I just shared with you:

> **R**ecognize that there is a problem: In the management meeting, we discussed that there was a problem with the picking process.
>
> **O**bserve the process: Seeing how the trainer was conducting the training gave me insight into multiple issues.
>
> **L**istening to what Russ said* to the trainees and how he was describing what they had to do to get around the issues led me to ideas for solving problems.
>
> **E**xploring the solutions with Russ and Joe made the solutions stronger and widely accepted by all.
>
> ***By the Way:** Asking Joe why the numbering system was changed gave me insight into the deeper problem of what happens when the person who is doing the actual work is not consulted or listened to.

OTHER TAKEAWAYS

- Color-coded labels make it easy to identify additional information, such as if there are multiple slots, not to open certain
  packing, to pick as one unit, and more. There are no limits
  to using labels to show better information.
- Express your opinion and be proactive. Your expertise, even
  when not in a particular department, might be exactly what
  is needed to resolve a problem.
- Nontechnical, inexpensive solutions can solve expensive
  problems.

CHAPTER 6

YOUR BEST MISTAKES CREATE INNOVATION

I remember a conversation that I had with my father. I had made some sort of mistake. I don't remember what. His response was "Did you learn from it?"

I said, "Yes."

He said, "Then it wasn't a mistake, it was a learning experience."

In 1994, we started a new line of business with a local deli food company. The purpose was to provide freshly made sandwiches with a longer shelf life for convenience stores. They looked wonderful. They tasted great!!! The best ingredients were used. The bread was awesome! My favorite was the cheese bread. It was a large sub roll with cheese on the top of it. It was so flavorful.

There was only one problem, and it was a major one: the bread would get moldy before its printed expiration date. Most of our customers had weekly deliveries, so they needed that length of shelf life. After trying to solve the problem for a few months, we closed that part of the division, at a cost of about $50,000. As I'll share later, we would eventually find a better approach for this product line.

Nonetheless, we all hate to make mistakes. What if you looked at what you consider mistakes as an evolutionary process? Consider that a mistake is truly an opportunity to learn and create better results.

I do not believe you can have a successful business or life if you do not make mistakes and learn from them. The true mistake is not learning to let go and move on.

Why was this sandwich lesson good for us? It was a real turning point in our strategy. Out of this came the realization that we needed to find the best product that we could distribute that met certain standards, such as:

- Excellent quality and taste
- Good value for the money
- A long enough shelf life

We found a supplier with great sandwiches that met our requirements, which we private-labeled under my niece Rachael's name. We expanded the Rachael's line to pastries, candy, salads, coffee, and other items over the years. The name Rachael's became synonymous with quality because of our high standards.

As we grew, our approach in reviewing the food items extended to all food items that we brought in: How is the taste? How is the packaging? And how will our market respond to it?

Fast-forward to 2008. We again were finding that the sandwiches we were distributing did not have a long enough shelf life. This was because of the manufacturing and delivery time. Our customers were demanding a longer shelf life. Food packaging had developed to a point that there was the capability to keep sandwiches fresh for longer periods of time. We decided that it was time to make our own sandwiches once again, so we built our own USDA-approved food manufacturing operation, Rachael's Food Corporation.

This time we hired someone who had a lot of experience in the fresh food manufacturing industry. We were very careful to bring ingredients in "just in time," so the sandwich ingredients were as fresh as possible.

Mike Pepin, VP of Rachael's Food Corp. and VP of Commissary Operations for NCD, says this:

We have two menus at Rachael's. The MAP (Modified Atmosphere Packaging) has a shelf life of 14 days and uses nitrogen to limit the amount of oxygen in the container. Bacteria need oxygen to grow; they grow at a stifled rate when foods are packaged this way, extending the shelf life. [Our parent company] buys this sandwich with 14 days but guarantees it for only 7 to the customer, so the buyers can purchase it based on projections and always have it in stock.

The shorter shelf-life product is packaged with a variety of containers and has a shelf life of five days. This, because of the short shelf life, is built based on the customers' orders. Customers need to order this product two days in advance to allow for production (built to order).

As you can see with Rachael's Food Corp., we were able to guarantee seven days on the shelf for some sandwiches because the technology to keep food fresh had advanced so much. It is always advantageous to explore good ideas that weren't successful, because there might be advances now that will make them successful.

We ship our freshly made food products to retailers on the day we make them. So, one benefit of making our own sandwiches and salads is that the next day, our employees can inexpensively buy what has not been sold to the retailers after the picking process is completed. We even make extra food for the break room to ensure our employees can have a good sandwich or salad if there is not enough left over.

We now produce a full line of salads, sandwiches, and entrees. Besides the convenience stores that we sell our brand to, we private-label for grocery stores, colleges, and some convenience store chains. This division is doing so well that we outgrew our production facility and expanded the current facility twice.

Through the years, I have seen changes in packaging as improvements happen all of the time. When we started with salads, it was one container. Now, there is the main container for the salad and a top plastic layer with compartments for different ingredients such as chicken, cheese, and so on; this separation keeps the salad fresh longer. In the yogurt parfait, there is packaging that keeps the granola separate from the yogurt.

We went full circle, from someone looking for the best product to private-label and sell, to a company that also creates the best product to private-label for others.

Mike Pepin started out as the Head of Security at J. Polep. My brother, Jeff, who had the benefit of lessons learned at the dinner table, recognized that Mike was able to fill a larger role.

Well before he became VP, Mike was asked to run the J. Polep satellite warehouse on Cape Cod. He was there for two years. He returned to our main location in Chicopee and got involved with the construction of the Rachael's site. When the person running Rachael's Food Corp. departed, Mike took over the operation. Because of his attention to detail and quality, Rachael's has expanded tremendously.

SEVEN PILLARS OF BUSINESS PROFITABILITY

The important lessons from turning mistakes into innovation are as follows . . .

1. Recognize that there is a problem.
    - Think about a problem that you had or have.
    - Is it an opportunity for improvement?
    - What can you or did you do to solve it?

2. Cut your losses. Cutting losses can be the big win.
   - Is it something you would be better off letting go of, that is, stop production, stop selling, stop doing?
3. Find a solution that works best in your business environment, or find how to create a new business model that your idea will work in.
   - Try again with a new strategy when the opportunity comes up. It could be years later, or immediately.
   - You know what did not work. You can use that knowledge to make it work, if it is still valuable for you to do so.
   - Don't fall in love with an idea; fall in love with the outcome you want and find the best way to accomplish it.
4. Just because something did not work in the past does not mean it cannot work with a new strategy.
   - What needs to change to make your idea work?
   - What are the best practices in the industry, and will they work for you?
5. Keep looking for ways to improve and expand.
   - Go to trade shows for your type of product or service. What is new that can help you?
   - What products can you develop?
   - What are your competitors doing that would be good for you to do?
6. Listen to your customers.
   - Our customers told us that they needed more shelf life. We listened and responded well.
7. Most importantly, mistakes are opportunities for learning.
   - What did you learn from your "mistake"?
   - What evolved from this experience?

A NEW KIND OF R.O.I.

Learning from your mistakes and creating better outcomes makes you a stronger, more profitable company.

What came out of this experience was a way to look at a situation — **R.O.I.**, or **Recognize, Optimize, Innovate**.

We **Recognized** that there was a problem and researched the best way to proceed.

We **Optimized** a solution, which was to find the best product to private-label that would meet our customers' needs.

When that stopped meeting the customers' needs, we **Recognized** the need for improvement and revisited creating our own sandwiches with the new technologies that were available.

Innovation came at all steps along the way. We were constantly innovating to create better outcomes and solutions. You can't have innovation if you are stuck on a hamster wheel. You have to be willing to let go of the outcome you wanted to create the outcome that you need.

My father certainly was right when he said there are no mistakes, just learning experiences. Rachael's Food Corp. was a very successful learning experience!

Don't let a situation where you fail deter you from trying again with the knowledge that you gained, better resources, and technology. You might just be missing out on an innovation that creates profitability for your company and sets you apart from others.

KEY TAKEAWAYS

Your process is the path to your profitability. Challenges are inevitable, but they are also an opportunity to create or continue your continuous improvements. As you observe and reflect on your process, don't forget the Seven Pillars of Business Profitability:

1. Recognize that there is a problem.

2. Cutting your losses can be the big win.
3. Find a solution that works best in your business environment, or find how to create a new business model that your idea will work in.
4. Just because something did not work in the past does not mean it cannot work with a new strategy.
5. Keep looking for ways to improve and expand.
6. Listen to your customers.
7. Most importantly, mistakes are opportunities for learning.

And finally, using the **R.O.I.** Strategy — Recognize, Optimize, Innovate — gives you the opportunity to create new solutions that are advantageous to your company.

CHAPTER 7

CREATING EFFICIENCIES FOR THE USER INCREASES PRODUCTIVITY AND PROFITABILITY

There is a massive cost in creating inefficient, hard-to-use programs. It has never been so apparent as it is now with the internet and being online, and it all has to do with programming. Good, user-friendly programming makes it easier for your employees to do their work, and it keeps your customers happy. I will explain more below in the 10 Seconds section.

When I arrived at Polep Candy and Tobacco Company, I decided that the best way to learn the business was to go into each department and see what the employees' workday was like. As I met with them, I would look at things like how many keystrokes it took to do a process. What I found was that many processes could be streamlined, some from five keystrokes down to two, and others eliminated entirely with proper coding.

Why was that important? Imagine that the employee was doing that 200 times a day. It certainly gets boring, and it increases the margin of error, especially when they are entering data, as they could lose their place. Each keystroke takes time. Eliminating keystrokes gives the employee more time to work on something else.

Another example was our month-end process. When the computer operators ran month-end reports, they had to enter dates. If they entered a date wrong, they would have to restore data. I created a simple program that displayed the dates and asked if they were correct. We never had that issue again, which made operations much more efficient. That idea came from a program I created at IBM.

IBM

During my training at IBM, I learned that multiple programming languages, numbering systems, and database designs were all critical and necessary to know. However, the one that had the most impact on me was Systems Analysis and Design. This taught me how to make my programs easy to use and was the most influential for me in my career because it gave me the right process to create great programming logic.

I thought that working at IBM would be so tough because of the truly difficult nine weeks of training. What I found was that they were very supportive and wanted to see you succeed. Although the nine weeks gave me a great foundation, IBM was continually educating us. If you think about it, technology changes so fast. Without continual education, one gets rusty quickly. Businesses need to implement new technology to maintain productivity and efficiency.

A few months after I started, I was asked to go see the VP of finance. Let's call him Richard. What Richard wanted to do was to look at information collected from the Worldwide Survey Database — which had resulted in an extremely large database of customer responses. He wanted to look at the data in field numbers 72–74. We didn't have field names back then, nor did we have an easy way of filtering information like we have today as in programs like Excel.

I went back to my desk and thought about it. I thought about how much information was in this survey and figured that Richard, inevitably, would be coming back to me to ask me to write another program to look at other details.

I remembered that in Job Control Language you could pass parameters to a program. I decided to try that. I was able to write the JCL so that it asked him, "What field would you like to start with?" and "What field would you like to end with?" Ironically, what seemed to be really hard to learn during the nine weeks of training I was able to apply and program in just a few hours. I won't get technical here, but it was a very unique way of coding back then.

Because of this, Richard was able to enter the field numbers himself. It solved his real business need because he could look at anything in that enormous database without waiting for another program to be written.

Then I wrote up the instructions in the manner taught to me by Paul Hunziker, my project manager: the KISS method (Keep it simple, Stupid) or the PhD method (Push here, Dummy). Both ways have served me well throughout my career.

I went to show Richard how to run this program. He was thrilled when I told him how I'd programmed it so that he could analyze any part of the Worldwide Survey Database. He had the biggest smile on his face.

By *Recognizing* that Richard would need to analyze other parts of the survey, and that having me continually create additional programs so that he could analyze another part of the survey would be very inefficient, I looked for a way to *Optimize* the process. Using the Job Control Language to pass the parameters was *Innovative*.

By providing this solution, Richard was happy and could be much more efficient, as he could choose what he needed whenever he needed it. There was no additional cost of having me write additional programs to analyze the Worldwide Survey Database. I received a letter of commendation for this program from him for creating an "innovative solution to an ongoing problem."

What I learned in the nine weeks of training — and from listening to my parents — about what could be improved helped me create an efficient solution and increased productivity, thereby decreasing costs.

10 SECONDS
(EFFICIENT AND USER-FRIENDLY PROGRAMMING
MAKES CUSTOMERS HAPPY)

Today, we have so much more exposure to inefficient programming. It is critical to understand this, as today a majority of our business is online. With so much competition out there, you have only a few seconds to keep someone interested in staying on your website or on your app. Websites and apps are all programs. The Neilsen Norman Group states that a person stays on a website for an average of ten seconds, so you need to get their interest immediately.[7] You have to keep their interest and have an easy-to-navigate website.

There are ways to build a program that is easy to navigate. A website can be built responsively so that it works on multiple platforms, such as PC, Mac, Android, and Apple tablets and phones. So many people are looking at websites when they are not near a computer, me included. Recently, I was looking at an email from a French pastry company. I was interested in seeing if they had a particular product but, as I was on my phone and the website hadn't been built "responsively," I could not see what I wanted, as the information did not fit on the page. Scrolling right and left was too cumbersome. Although I love their products, I left the site. Will I look at it on my computer? Possibly. If it is important enough, yes. But they lost the impulse sale.

Online ordering (via website or application) and report generation have become critical for companies such as distribution companies, where customers want to be able to order using a computer or mobile app. They want to be able to place an order easily. They don't want to go to multiple screens to do so. They might want to see what they ordered last time and how well a product is doing. All of this is possible on multiple platforms when thoughtful design is

---

[7]   Nielsen, Jakob, "How Long Do Users Stay on Web Pages?" *Nielsen Norman Group,* September 11, 2011 (website).

used. The biggest questions: How will the customer be using this? What do they want to see? What is valuable to them? You can get all of this information by asking the customers.

As mentioned in Chapter 2, we created a focus group that went to customers in order to discover what they needed. How could we help them become better companies? By improving your customers' experiences, you make yourself a better, more profitable company — with loyal customers. They want to be your customer because you make it easy for them to do business with you.

Creating efficiency reduces costs and increases productivity. The time spent on creating a great customer experience saves you time and money as you develop solutions right the first time. Creating a great customer experience makes a happy, loyal, and profitable customer. Customers come back to you as you recognize their needs and develop solutions tailored to them.

KEY TAKEAWAYS

- Creating easy-to-use programs and websites increases your users' efficiency and profitability. This includes your internal and external use programs.
- You have ten seconds or less to capture someone's attention on your website. Get your message across without them having to scroll down
- Keeping someone on your website means you need to have easy navigation, otherwise they will go somewhere else.
- A customer comes back to an easy-to-use website where they can quickly attain the information they need.
- When creating a website, hire someone who understands your message and make sure that it is programmed responsively well (i.e., it can be easily viewed on an iPhone, iPad, computer, tablet, any of the major browsers, etc.), no matter the size of the screen.

CHAPTER 8

GETTING BETTER RESULTS WITH CROSS-FUNCTIONAL TEAMS

Creating a cross-functional team is critical for many projects. One project that required an extensive team from most areas of the company was when Massachusetts passed its Compliance Law (Privacy Law). We had to write security protocols and create a Written Information Security Program.

NAVIGATING THE CHANGES NEEDED TO CREATE A SECURITY PROGRAM

In 2009, we learned about the massive changes to Privacy Laws. After attending a few seminars about this, I realized that if we did this the wrong way, it would open us up to lawsuits and fines, and we would have to encrypt so much information on our iSeries computer that it could cause us significant problems. The major problem would be if we had to restore the system to another system.

The private information on our computers and on paper included data such as social security numbers, banking information, charge card information, and driver's licenses. We had private information in many different departments. This project became a massive process improvement effort because we had to determine what was needed and what was not.

It is essential to create a team of people from all departments that will be affected by the changes because they know their daily routines. They understand how the changes would affect how they do business. I always depend on the people doing the job to be the experts. They will offer suggestions that I would never have thought of.

In this instance, I spoke about the scope of the project at a management meeting. I asked who should be on this cross-functional team. We all decided upon these areas: Accounts Receivable, Accounts Payable, Customer Service, Information Technology, Sales, Human Resources, Transportation, the CFO, and the VP of Administration. As private information could be used by any of these departments, we had to go through all of their processes and change what we needed to so that the private information was safe. The cross-functional team started with more people, but when this law didn't affect a department, those people would attend only the meetings that affected their department, even if tangentially.

THE CRITICAL NATURE OF A CROSS-FUNCTIONAL TEAM

It is crucial to identify who should attend meetings early, as productivity increases by having the right people attend.

The real benefit of this project was finding out that there were things that we were doing because we had always done it that way. Wow!!! Every company should go through processes every year, just to see what they are doing that they do not need to do anymore. "We have always done it that way" can be a money pit.

We went through, department by department, discovering why they had to collect the information and where and how the information was being used. A major benefit of having the CFO at these meetings was that decisions could be made immediately about changing processes.

Here is some of what we discovered and how we resolved issues. (Please note: this represented months of meeting once a week as we were doing deep dives into processes, finding any issues, and creating new processes or solutions.)

TRANSPORTATION DEPARTMENT

Meeting Attendees: Director of Transportation, Director of HR, CFO, IT, CIO

Problem: Information, including driver's license numbers, had to be emailed to our fleet management company. Then the information had to be stored.

Resolution: We got the department some encryption software to use when sending private information. For storage of hard copies, we bought them a locked cabinet that they kept in a locked office.

ACCOUNTS RECEIVABLE DEPARTMENT

Meeting Attendees: Director of transportation, director of HR, CFO, IT, CIO, director of A/R, VP of sales

Problem 1: Credit applications contained private information.

Resolution: We put locks on cabinets and kept the keys in an office that is locked at night.

Problem 2: Some customers pay by credit card. As there are so few transactions, after processing, the backup information is kept in a locked box in an office and shredded after a month.

Resolution: Use encryption software when sending private data. A cross-shredder was purchased so that they could easily shred documents that contained private data. A cross-shredder is important so that someone cannot piece together a document.

ACCOUNTS PAYABLE DEPARTMENT

Meeting Attendees: Initially, the A/P manager, the CFO, IT, and the CIO attended.

Problem and Resolution: Nothing was necessary.

SALES DEPARTMENT

Meeting Attendees: CFO, director of A/R, VP of sales, IT, CIO
   Problem: Credit applications include private data.
   Resolution: Salespeople fill out the credit applications on their iPad; J. Polep's email service has its own built-in encryption. (We were using a third-party application before.) During our discussion, we found that some information on our main computer was unnecessary. There were other ways to handle it, so we took the information off.

CUSTOMER SERVICE DEPARTMENT

Meeting Attendees: Initially, the customer service manager, the CFO, IT, and the CIO attended.
   Problem and Resolution: No issues. Customer Service departments in other companies deal with private information, such as credit cards, debit cards, checking information, and more. This is why it is important to have discovery sessions with each department.

HUMAN RESOURCES DEPARTMENT

Meeting Attendees: CFO, director of HR, IT, CIO
   Problem: This was the big one for us, as they have so much private information. Social security numbers were used everywhere, including job applications.
   Resolution: We removed the social security number box from the job applications, as it is only needed if someone is hired. We also installed locked cabinets to hold all paperwork that contains private information. They are kept in a locked room.

INFORMATION TECHNOLOGY DEPARTMENT

Meeting Attendees: CFO, IT, CIO, VP of sales (Sales was involved because a lot of the information appearing on reports was from reports they requested.)

Problem: This was the most extensive review, as there was information on the computer that we had to deal with, and we had to provide additional layers of security.

Resolution: There was some information carried for some reports that we were able to take off, or we determined that it was public information, so it was not a problem.

SECURITY — PART OF IT

Attendees: CFO, director of A/R, IT, CIO

Problem: Keeping passwords secure.

Resolution: In IT, we put in some standards for changing passwords every 90 days and automatically needing to sign in again if your computer was idle for 15 minutes. I used software to help us write each security policy together and the WISP. Different departments deal with different information. Someone working as an order selector doesn't have access to confidential information, so they might not need the Confidential Information Policy.

CONSIDERATIONS FOR YOUR WRITTEN INFORMATION SECURITY POLICY AND ADDITIONAL SECURITY POLICIES.

You must determine what policies you need for your business. My recommendation is that if you are in multiple states, you put your WISP and additional security policies together that take into account the requirements for all states. If not, it will be too hard to keep control of it.

This should be revisited every six months to see if any changes have occurred that would require you to either take new precautions or write something else into the WISP and the additional security policies.

One way to keep on top of this would be to create a form to be filled out to indicate if personal information needs to be used in a new report, used in a new program, or kept in a new file on the computer.

Be aware that your third-party vendors need to give you their privacy policy. We had to collect such information from our vendors when we created these policies. You have to know how they protect your data when using third-party vendors that access your information or if your information is stored off-site. Make sure that you have wording in all contracts that ensures your information remains yours, and have a removal policy in place with them in case you decide to move to a new vendor. That is always negotiated upfront, **before you sign the contract**. Verify that it is in the contract before you sign it, as something can be missed.

Also, it is important that the vendor can't supersede what is in your contract by asking you, as a user, to agree to changes online in order to use the software. With Microsoft 365, Adobe, and other mass-market software, you can't say no to accepting the updated agreement; if you say no, you will not be able to use the software. The software that I am talking about is not mass-market.

Putting the time in upfront when negotiating a contract will save you so much money in the event the software doesn't work, give you protections against changes to their online software agreement, provide performance metrics, and more.

Part of the Massachusetts Compliance Law is security, such as having good antivirus software. Your own state or states that you service will have that detailed in their privacy laws.

Stay cognizant of changes to these Privacy or Compliance Laws. As they change, you might have to change your security policies and how you operate.

EXPENSIVE WRONGS

When we originally put in security protections, we only had antivirus software and a firewall. Today we are using a suite of products from Sophos for even higher levels of security. There are so many companies that have security software — and sometimes hardware — that you must do an in-depth analysis. This takes time. I had an IT team working with me to determine which program was the best and at what cost. Because Cybersecurity is such a significant issue, I cover it in more detail in Chapter 11 (A Shocking Evolution).

This was just a brief overview of what we had to be aware of and what we had to change at the time the Privacy Laws were implemented. Today there are companies that will help you through the process. I advocate using a company that specializes in this unless you have your own well-trained security officer (CISO). Even then, it is a good idea to have someone else look at it. We don't know what we don't know.

The cost of getting this wrong is high. There are fines, loss of reputation, loss of customers, and the huge cost of correcting the problem.

Having a cross-functional team to determine the best strategy gave us the opportunity for the best outcome for the company. Cross-functional teams create better solutions because of the knowledge that the people bring from their departments. They can help determine the impact changes will have on the company. Better solutions are created by dialogue.

KEY TAKEAWAYS

- Choosing the right people to be part of the cross-functional team is critical to the success of the project.
- Cross-functional teams create better, stronger solutions because of the knowledge members bring to the team.
- Dialogue creates better solutions, which increases efficiency and profitability.
- Projects often need to be revisited and refined.
- Mitigating risk increases profitability by way of eliminating potential mistakes.
- Compliance and Privacy Laws are continually changing. Not being up to date can cost money, and also credibility, if you have a breach.

CHAPTER 9

CONTINUOUS IMPROVEMENT

Process Improvement and Technology are the greatest marriage. I think that continuous improvement is the key to the greatest advancements both in technology and process improvement.

In this chapter, I discuss the unbelievable opportunities that have evolved because of the massive increase in a computer's storage, processing speed, and battery size. Just the pizza box discussion below will impress upon you the massive difference that only forty years made.

When I started in the family business in 1980, I got there just as they were implementing a new computer system, the IBM System 34. The previous system, the IBM System 3, which was an early midrange computer, used a disk storage system that was comprised of four 2.5-megabyte disks. Two of those were removable. Removable disks allowed the company to process more information.

For instance, Accounts Receivable, Order Entry, and Accounts Payable would all be run as separate programs, with the files for each one on a swappable disk. I do remember visiting one time and watching these departments change the disk over to another program. I am sure that it made for an interesting time and a lot of planning when running month-end or year-end programs.

The System 34 was much better than the System 3 as the System 34 had a floppy drive (which processes data faster) rather than a punch card reader (which would involve inputting the data manually onto the card, leaving too much room for error). The floppy drive was much more efficient and took up much less space. Plus, there were a lot fewer typing errors.

The keypunch operators were able to key the order onto a floppy disk. Then they would bring it over to the System 34 to be processed. That continued through many years and several computer systems until we finally went to using CRTs (think of computer screens) for data entry.

Our IBM System 34 had less than 100 megabytes, and you did not have to swap disks. You could have enough storage right on the computer. We were running two businesses off that system. I remember my father saying that we would never grow out of it. Famous last words. Two years later, we were adding disk space. We upgraded to the newer, faster IBM System 36 in 1984.

We were growing so fast that we upgraded computer systems every three to five years. They became less expensive while geometrically increasing their capabilities. Our first AS/400, which we bought in 1989, had 4 gigabytes (GB) of storage on it and was so much faster than the previous systems. It even had a battery that was part of the system that would keep the system running for 20 minutes. When the power would go out, it gave us a few minutes to shut the computer down properly. What was truly impressive was that it was the size of a two-drawer filing cabinet.

What I want to make a point of is that smartphones today that fit in the palm of your hand have much more storage than the System 3 or the 34 and even the first AS/400. The first iPhone offered 4 GBs as its starting storage with an 8 GB max in 2007.[8] Today's smartphones and tablets have more onboard storage and processing speed than the midrange computers and mainframes of that time period. And they don't always need to be connected by wire to a power source.

---

[8] Cohen, Peter, "Macworld Expo Keynote Live Update: Introducing the iPhone," *Macworld,* January 9, 2007. Archived from the original on July 24, 2018. Retrieved September 4, 2020.

The disks on the System 3 were 18 inches in diameter and two inches high.

I have 256 GBs on my iPhone. That is equal to 102,400 of the System 3 disks.

I read that twenty thousand 18-inch pizzas would fill a football field.[9] *Five football fields to equal the storage on my iPhone!* Why is that important? It is important because of the power that we now hold in our hands and can put in our customers' and employees' hands.

*Pizza Box Calculation from Bedtime Math
(courtesy of Sandy LoPiccolo)*
"We divided the area of a football field — 57,600 square feet when you count the end zones, 48,000 square feet when you don't count the end zones — by the 2.25 square foot area of an 18-inch pizza box. That would give either 25,600 pizzas or 21,333 pizzas. We rounded down to be safe, and to have a better math question for the age level."

TECHNOLOGICAL DEVELOPMENTS AND ADVANCEMENTS

In 1980, my first major project was to bring in mobile computing using an MSI handheld unit that had very simple programming. It looked a lot like a calculator. My salespeople nicknamed it The Brick because of its size. They would have to connect an adapter to a phone to send the order to a computer. To us, it was extremely powerful. It gave us so much flexibility because the salespeople used to have to call their orders in to the customer service department or drop off the paper copies to be keyed in. The unit itself was 8

---

[9] "A Football Field of Pizza," *Bedtime Math Foundation* (online).

kilobytes, which equals 8,192 bytes (characters). The units cost us $2,400 each.

In 1982, we were able to go to faster, smaller, less expensive machines — the Telxon units for $500. They were about 4 × 6 inches. We were able to get many customers onto that technology as we were able to make a separate program for customers. We were able to take inventory using the Telxon units, making it much faster. These units also became a fallback for me when our main computer was down. Although it didn't happen often, we were able to keep on top of orders because the customer service reps would put the orders into the Telxon units. The receiving program we had for both the salespeople and customers would store all of the orders on its hard drive. And when our main computer was back up, the orders would be sent from the order-receiving computer to our main computer to be processed.

As storage got cheaper and processing speed got faster, we upgraded to new machines that could do more. Faster handhelds could handle more intricate programming. By 2005, these units had cellular and wireless capabilities. Our salespeople had much more information available to them on their devices and did not have to find a phone to send their orders.

For our warehouse, we developed inventory receiving and put-away programs using ruggedized handhelds. They were able to connect to the iSeries via the wireless network, so information was passed and updated almost instantly. No longer did they have to write down what they did and input it into the computer later. They were able to key or scan the information into the handheld, which also gave them immediate verification. Much more efficient and also a massive reduction in errors.

A truly remarkable change came with smartphones and tablets. The amount of information that can be accessed and processed today by our salespeople and by our customers is mind-blowing to me. I walked into a customer's location several years ago, and he was on his iPhone accessing information about his orders. He told me how much he loved having the capability on his phone. The fact that all of this processing could be done over the cellular network was very freeing. He could be anywhere in the world and still check this information.

The other major development was the ability to make batteries smaller. My father's first car phone, because of the battery, was about the size of a small carry-on bag ($12 \times 12 \times 8$ inches) and weighed a good 15 pounds. I think that the battery was good for about 15 minutes, so we always kept it plugged into the cigarette charger. The phone itself was about the size of a brick. Today we complain when our phones don't hold a charge for a day.

There are four examples of continuous improvement here.

1. Decreasing the size of storage while increasing the quantity of storage.
2. Decreasing the size of batteries and increasing the time they are available for use.
3. Expanding capability to communicate wirelessly.
4. Increasing the processing speed. As both the battery size and storage decreased in size and increased in capability, the processing speed increased geometrically.

What a smartphone or tablet can do today with the programs that are available far exceeds the capabilities of a mainframe computer that was in use just 30 to 40 years ago.

To put it in perspective, the first iPhone was released in 2007. The most storage that you could have was 8 GB. On the iPhone 14, you can have a terabyte (TB).

Not Quite Peace on Earth . . .
(The Impact of the Southwest Airlines Debacle)

Southwest Airlines probably had great software when they implemented it in 2006. As a reference point, the first iPhone came out in 2007. Unfortunately, Southwest didn't listen to their employees and unions who started complaining about the crew scheduling systems and software around 2015.[10]

As many of you may already know, their lack of improvement presented a mess just in time for the holidays in 2022. Customers were more than inconvenienced — they were scattered about the country with nowhere to go. People missed time with family, they were unavailable for work they couldn't afford to miss, and they were stressed out during a time when we hope to experience peace and comfort.

Southwest said this mess would cost them more than $1 billion.[11] This loss, along with the holiday debacle, was avoidable. In 2023, Southwest said that they spend $1 billion on technology a year. I would want to know where these dollars are going and why the systems haven't been upgraded to new technology.

Do they have continuous improvement in place? If so, who is on that team? Certainly not the employees or the union, which said there was a problem with the software.

A knowledgeable team would recognize that a system could only be improved so much. They should also have been on top of what new software was available. It is important to know what is available so that you can improve your company's infrastructure before the software becomes obsolete.

---

[10] Paul, Andrew, "You Can Blame Southwest Airlines' Holiday Catastrophe on Outdated Software," *Popular Science* — Recurrent, January 3, 2023.

[11] Glascock, Taylor, "Southwest Says Holiday Meltdown Will Cost It More Than $1 Billion," *New York Times*, January 26, 2023.

> Don't be like Southwest. Listen to your employees. Improve your infrastructure — before you have major issues, unhappy customers, and enormous losses.

MULTILEVEL BENEFITS OF TECHNOLOGICAL DEVELOPMENT

The development of technology to date allows for greater productivity. Everything I spoke about here was originally done using paper and multiple people versus going directly into the computer.

- Customers can look up a lot of information easily instead of calling.
- Customers can create their own orders instead of calling in their order or waiting for a salesperson to come.
- Salespeople have all of the specials right on their tablets.
- Salespeople can also assess how well their customer is doing with a sales promotion.
- Errors are reduced as information is verified instantaneously.

The capabilities of smartphones and tablets have opened us up to better, faster, and more efficient ways to conduct business. What we call midrange or mainframe computers — along with desktop and laptop computers — also have had the same exponential growth in capabilities and decrease in costs because of the improvements in technology.

Communication technologies keep us connected and allow us much more flexibility in how we conduct business.

I haven't even covered here what the development of the PC did for business. The PC and the Mac both are examples of how technology helped businesses, especially small businesses, that never would have been able to afford computer systems. And with all of the programs that have been developed for the PC and Mac, all businesses have seen an increase in productivity. The PC and the Mac are excellent examples of continuous improvement.

This chapter's exploration of technology's continuous improvement began in 1980. Over the course of the 45 years leading to the publishing of my book, I hope you can see the evolution and effect of technology. It is critical that you stay on top of these developments and harness the power of these advancements to achieve a more profitable and efficient business.

As technology improves, there is also further opportunity for your programs, systems, communication, concepts, and services to continually improve as well.

KEY TAKEAWAYS

- Not improving your technology puts your business at risk for unnecessary costs or even crumbling down altogether.
- Continuous improvement is often both technology and process improvement.
- Implementing improvements to technology, along with process improvement, is critical to keeping your company at the forefront of your industry.
- Providing technology that increases your customer's productivity and satisfaction is critical. This is part of the service that you provide that makes you stand out from others.
- A well-written program that helps your employee complete tasks faster and more efficiently decreases costs and increases productivity.
- Aging systems will eventually become a detriment as they don't have the capability of using the current processing speeds, communication protocols, and hardware platforms available. A company will need to look at replacing software and hardware as technology, and their business, become more sophisticated.
- Ensuring that your company has the best possible solutions will increase profitability because of increased productivity and efficiency.

CHAPTER 10

TECHNOLOGY: THE GOOD, THE BAD, AND THE UGLY

I remember my father complaining about the new computer system that he bought. It was a challenging transition, and the consultants were difficult to work with. It was taking a lot longer and costing a lot more to go to this new computer system than he had planned for. He said that one day he drove down to the river to pick out a spot to throw the computer into.

I think that this was the story that made me choose to work for IBM, because I felt that computers should be a help, not a hindrance.

There are so many horror stories of companies having major issues when going to a new system.

I remember when the Hershey Company was going to a new Enterprise Resource Planning software system that would replace its current software system. It is software that runs all aspects of the business including order processing, deliveries, accounts payable, accounts receivable, possibly purchasing, and more. It is software that runs every aspect of the business. If there were programs required, such as the routing software that we use, the systems would have to talk to each other. They chose Enterprise Resource Planning software by a well-known company, SAP, to replace their then-current software. It was 1999. When they flipped the switch, they were unable to deliver the candy. I remember this, as Hershey's was one of our biggest vendors, and we were out of stock of their products. If they had tested enough, they could have avoided this. I read an article that said they spent $112 million dollars on the system and had $100 million in lost sales.[12] They recovered from this. Most companies can't.

There was a large company that was local to me. They had bought and refurbished a very large building with new conveyors and a new software system. When they went live with the new system, they could not handle the orders or deliver products. Unfortunately, they went out of business. To me, it was really sad as they were a really good family-owned company that employed many in the area. I made a vow that this would not happen to us.

TECHNOLOGY CAN MAKE OR BREAK YOUR COMPANY

The right software can make you more efficient and more profitable. However, the wrong software can put you out of business. Choosing the right software at the right price and with the right support takes due diligence and cross-functional teams to review the software.

Cross-functional teams can help determine how well the software works for your company. You may ask yourself: Does the software fit your business, or do you have to create a lot of custom software? Creating custom software is expensive, and you have to update it at a great cost when there is a software update. If the file structures remain the same, then you can often make the transition to the newer version fairly easily.

Alternatively, we need to be careful with creating too much customization because companies often get locked into older versions of software. It defeats the purpose of buying the new software in the first place as you can't get the enhancements and improvements to the system that you spent so much money on.

---

[12] Gross, Jonathan, "A Case Study on Hershey's ERP Implementation Failure: The Importance of Testing and Scheduling," *Pemeco Consulting*, April 25, 2019 (website).

Be aware that file structures can change with new releases of the software, so what is true today might not be true in the future — no matter what you were promised.

When you move to a new software system, the software will do things differently. Understanding the changes that you will need to make to have the software work for you is critical so that you can be functional when you go live. This includes an evaluation of reports and the programs that were created by your employees and additional software that connects to your software system.

How will you accomplish servicing your customers with reports that they are used to receiving? Understanding what reports are available in the software is key. It will save you a lot of time versus recreating reports. If the report isn't available, where will you get the information that you need to continue to produce these reports, and how long will the process take you to do?

If you are keeping certain systems that have to "talk" to the new system, how is that going to be accomplished? When someone selling you the system says that they will write an API, which means a programming interface, make sure that they are aware of exactly how you use that software and the impact on you if it doesn't work. Think of the Hershey situation. All systems have to pass information back and forth efficiently, without errors, in order for you to operate from Day 1 of your go-live date.

PROCESS IMPROVEMENT IS ALWAYS PART OF THE PLAN

A major reason that process improvement is so important is that a new system will be faster. Bringing over bad processes to a new system just makes the inefficient processes faster and creates a greater loss. Since a new system should make a company more efficient, you must look at the way something is being done in the new system and make it work for you. This means having the people involved who would need to evaluate how the new functionality would work for the business. They have to own the new process, so let them voice their concerns so that they can create the change needed. Sometimes it is just letting them know the cost of changing the software that has them embrace the change.

How well does your company embrace change? Embracing change is critical to the success of new technology. One of the reasons my change process included cross-functional teams was so every area would have a voice in the process. Concerns have been discussed. The teams have been shown how the new software will accomplish what they are currently doing today. If a process isn't handled, they will discuss how they will be able to get the result they want and if it is critical, will they need some customized software? When people are heard and enough time is spent on the change effort, there is less fear, and every area has a champion from their department for the new software.

Another key element to this change process and implementation of the new system is who are you going to pick to lead and manage this project? Have they ever done a project of this size before? A large project will require a team. The project director needs to be able to plan and organize the people and the strategy for implementation. The team needs a leader who can make tough decisions such as the need to delay a go-live date for various reasons.

There is a much greater cost to going live and failing versus delaying. For instance, in 2019 we replaced our phone system, which consisted of 400 lines (200 on-site extensions and 200 voicemail only). It was my responsibility to manage that project from creating the cross-functional team to look at phone systems, to making sure that the functionality that we needed was in there, and to ensure that when we went live we were fully operational. This included running new wires for the network to handle the new system.

I had to delay it twice. Once when the network administrator found that there was a recall for the network switches. Think of network switches like the traffic lights that were all through the 300,000 square feet of the warehouse. The good news: it was free to replace them. The bad news was that to replace them, we had to get up 30 feet in the air in some areas, and they were hard to get to in others. We were supposed to go live in mid-December. Because of other projects and the holidays, we put it off till January of 2018. Then, there was another issue with implementation due to another network problem. I have to admit, I was frustrated as this one should have been caught by a person on my team when we were initially looking at specifications. As we all depend on other people to do their job correctly, this can happen no matter how often you go over the details.

The look on his face showed that he knew he'd made an error. The good news is that *we found it in the testing phase.* I asked him, "How long until this gets fixed?" Even though it wasn't a long time, we had to delay the go-live date again until March due to other projects.

The hard part for me was telling everyone that we had to delay it again. That is why the person running the project has to be strong. Many of the stakeholders won't understand the delay. It has to be explained properly. The right decisions have to be made to have a successful implementation and go-live date. The key is to also insist on testing, testing, testing.

TEST, TEST, TEST

Testing is what makes for a smooth transition to a new system and also to ensure that incremental changes do not cause operational problems. When replacing our ERP system, which we did three times, I made a flow chart of how orders came into the system and how they were processed through the system, including our external systems. We tested until we all felt comfortable that we could go live. We would save our orders for the day and run them through the new system in a way that we would be able to make sure that all of the programs, such as our purchasing program, our warehouse system, and our routing program, integrated properly with the new system. This included our order selection process, the orders getting onto the right truck, and with the right delivery information. Of course, all the financials were checked to ensure that the information was being updated properly.

If you have another type of business, you will test everything that you need to function in your business. A pizza shop needs its inventory. They need to make sales and take payments. A doctor's office has to get people in and out; they have to bill insurance companies and collect co-pays. They have patients' records. All of that information has to be transferred into the new system, and the functions have to be tested.

THE IMPORTANCE OF TRAINING

What, besides planning and testing, is critical to a successful implementation? Training. The better you train, the more knowledgeable the user is and the more comfortable they are with the system. Some of that training will come during the testing process. I learned early on to take the best people from each department or job function and train them. They then train the others. They are able to explain the way to do something in the new system based upon their knowledge of the old system. They call this method "Train the trainer."

When training, I always had a list of what people needed to know to do their job function. Later on, that became an assessment sheet, so we knew we trained them on what they needed to know.

People felt comfortable with the training, as we had it on a separate system where they knew that they could practice as time allowed. With functions like order entry, accounts receivable, accounts payable, and so on, after the initial training, the department manager would set up times for them to practice on the new system. It is important that every person is well trained, including the people picking orders, putting away product, and doing other jobs. This makes people much more confident, efficient, and productive on Day 1.

PREPARE YOUR CUSTOMERS

I guarantee you that you won't think of everything for your go-live date. It is critical to prepare your customers for the new system. They need to know that there might be some issues and delays. One way to streamline this would be to have numbers that people can call for help. Different ones for internal users and customers with a team trained to help with issues that come up if your company is large enough. Why separate numbers? So the person who is best trained to answer the question will pick up the phone.

Make sure that the consultant or company that you used for your system is there and has allowed enough time to be there to help at the go-live day and beyond. With a system our size, there were multiple consultants available at our location to help answer questions. Having a team ready to respond to any issues helps with the transition.

Whatever business you have, whether you are a doctor's office, a restaurant, a hair salon, a store, or any place of business that requires a computer system, all I hear whenever someone goes to a new system is how tough it is.

Remember that what we call smartphones are basically small computer systems that have more power than the first computers and the first PCs. The ability to have powerful software literally in our hands has changed how we do business today.

The more complicated the systems that you are coming from and are going to, no matter what platform you choose, means that every step is longer and more in-depth. The time that you put in at each step will come back to you, as will the time that you don't put in. When we took the phone system live, we were immediately operational with just some minor adjustments. When we created mobile solutions, they got better and more powerful as mobile technology became more powerful. When we went "live" with ERP and other systems, there was always some work that had to be done to create reports that had been overlooked. That will always happen. The important part is to mitigate those issues by doing as much work upfront as possible. The critical point is that your company is operational without any issues that stop you from doing business and create more expenses. After all, you are going to the new system to increase profitability, increase efficiency, and to help your company with sustainable growth.

KEY TAKEAWAYS

- Review multiple systems with a cross-functional team.
- Spend enough time reviewing a system before signing a contract.
- Learn the capabilities of the new system before making changes. Often, the new system will have a different way of doing the same thing that you were doing. This deep dive would be done before the go-live date as there are functions that you need to stay in business.
- Too much customization of software locks you into old versions as you can't easily upgrade.
- Bringing over bad processes to a new system just makes inefficient processes faster and creates a greater loss.
- Testing and training are major elements in the success of implementing new systems and for incremental changes.
- The wrong choice will cost a lot of money and might put you out of business.
- Choosing the right system will increase profitability, increase efficiency, and will help your company with sustainable growth.

11

A SHOCKING EVOLUTION (CLOUD, ARTIFICIAL INTELLIGENCE, MACHINE LEARNING, AND CYBERSECURITY — UNDERSTANDING THE BUZZWORDS)

When I was at IBM, we had to send a program I had written to Paris. It was sent via satellite. Now, that was very impressive to me. If it cost several dollars a minute for a long-distance call in 1978, imagine the expense for sending data by satellite.

Today, tremendous opportunities have opened up to us because of the capabilities of computers, the internet, faster processing speeds, extremely fast communication lines, and easy connectivity. Unfortunately, these opportunities have also allowed for increased Cyberattacks.

There are so many new buzzwords that we hear today, such as cloud computing, AI, machine learning, and Cybersecurity. What do these words mean, and how do they affect your business? How can you use these capabilities to create a better business? How do you make sense of intangible data? How do you protect yourself from phishing and ransomware, along with other situations?

This chapter will provide you with some of those answers, and you will learn to ask more questions.

CLOUD COMPUTING AND
STORAGE: PROS AND CONS

As to the cloud, I can assure you that your data is not in space. Cloud is just a sexy name for your information residing on servers (computers) elsewhere. Many companies are relying on companies whose programs and data are "in the cloud" for at least some or all of their computer and software needs.

This makes sense in most cases. The choice of having your programs and computers onsite or in the cloud is up to you and the software that you are running. Sometimes the best software for your company will only be in the cloud. When we were looking at phone systems we had the option to choose onsite only, VoIP (Voice over Internet Protocol), or a combination. I chose a combination for the business as that was the most logical for us. When a remote location's internet was down, it took just a few minutes to reroute their calls to our main number. That is powerful.

Some questions that you must ask to determine your best option for a cloud solution are:

a) How long can I afford to be down for if the communications lines are down?
b) Does the provider have a high-availability solution in place? Meaning that if one site is not working, do they have an alternative site that is already running?
c) What is the security protocol that they have in place to protect my data?
d) If I leave them, what happens to my data?

It is critical that you have all of the above in your contract with your providers. It is also critical that nothing supersedes your contract, such as when they ask you online to accept the new terms and conditions or else you can't use the program.[13] Frankly, who reads every line of those when you want to use a program? I do try.

I like hybrid systems where I can have a system that will work onsite and one that can also work in the cloud. That is becoming less of an option over time as many systems are now being built to reside only in the cloud, which makes sense in many cases.

As more software is written to be on the cloud servers, it opens businesses up to more robust software because the cost of developing that software has been shared by many companies. This includes software that has the added capabilities of AI and machine learning.

ARTIFICIAL INTELLIGENCE AND MACHINE LEARNING

Artificial intelligence and machine learning is a fascinating topic to me, as there are so many opportunities here. There are many levels of AI and machine learning. Some you are already familiar with and are using already.

When you move an email to spam, you are telling your email program to automatically move emails from this sender to spam in the future. As you move more emails into spam, you create a database of senders that you do not want to hear from. The email application is programmed to look at that list and put those emails into your spam folder.

There are programs that will do that for you. The software will look at what is coming in and filter it. That software already has a repository of websites that are proven to be hackers. The software will also look to see if a message looks like it came unsolicited, mark it spam, and put it into your spam folder.

The problem can be that it was an email that you wanted, so in the initial process of using a program like this, check your spam folder daily to see if an email that you wanted is in there.

---

[13] Overly, Michael R., Karlyn, Matthew A., *A Guide to IT Contracting*, (Boca Raton, FL: CRC Press, 2013) Pg 24.

When you say that it wasn't spam, you then are training the machine to let those emails through. This type of system also stops phishing emails that look like they contain a real URL but is a false address. Think of the emails you might get that look like they are from Amazon or a bank. Or they might look like they come from your boss, asking you to transfer money. That did happen to us. Luckily, there were procedures in place to call first, versus send money. Plus, we had used a security awareness program, KnowBe4, to train people on phishing emails.

One of my favorite inventions is one many cars are installed with: safety features such as lane assist. My steering wheel starts shaking when I go over a line without my blinker on. The automobile company put sensors in the car that can "see" the lines and programmed the car to let the driver know that they are drifting over the line. Yet that doesn't compare to self-driving cars.

In Pennsylvania, in September of 2021, a man was driving his pregnant wife to the hospital in his Tesla. He decided to put the car on autopilot so that he could help his wife with only one hand on the wheel. As they pulled into the hospital, the baby was born! Elon Musk probably didn't envision this when he created the self-driving car, but what an incredible outcome![14]

Even travel is becoming easier because of AI. I was trying to buy some shoes at this small store in France. The saleswoman did not speak English, and my knowledge of French was inadequate. I call what I know "Restaurant French." I pulled out my cell phone and used the translation software. The saleswoman had an astonished look on her face. She commented, *"Mon Dieu!"* I left with the pair of shoes I wanted. We both were smiling at the end of the transaction. So much easier than pulling out my French-English dictionary!

The translation software has an extensive database of words in many languages. It makes it so much easier to travel. Although, I do

---

[14] Goldstein, Joelle, "Nurses Call This Newborn the 'Tesla Baby' After Mom Gave Birth While the Car Was in Autopilot," *People Magazine*, December 16, 2021 (website).

advise learning some basic words of the country that you are traveling to, as it is respectful, and it is appreciated.

Translation software is another example of AI. When you translate English to French, the program looks at a database to do that.

The use of chatbots for customer service has become much more prevalent. How often have you been on a site trying to solve a problem and it asks if you want to chat? Unless you have a really simple question for the chatbot that is easily found in their database, try to call. And then, try not to get frustrated when it takes you forever to get to a representative after pushing so many buttons and, finally, ending up screaming "representative" fifteen times. Yes, I am guilty of that. Luckily, machines don't have feelings. When I do get to a representative, I have to remind myself that I am now talking to a human being who did not develop this atrocious, customer-alienating software. By the way, that software did not have to be created that way. It could have been created in a very customer-centric way. That takes more thought and time.

Where AI really helps is when you want to search the internet for a product for the best price. I still find it hard to believe that I can get so many options from so many different places within a split second. The better you ask the question, the better information you get; that is, asking for a 65 inch TV will give all different brands. Add the name of the brand you want, and you will get more streamlined information. Add a store name, and you will see what that store has for 65 inch Samsung TVs. Just as with anything, you have to ask the right question to get the right result.

A sometimes annoying feature of the internet is when you search for something such as "Best places to visit in Italy" or "65 inch HD TVs" or anything else, then you see ads everywhere you go on the internet. Best Buy collected the information, put it into their marketing program, and used it to try to sell things to you. It is the price we pay for having easy access to information, as companies then have access to what we like.

Clicking on an ad will get you even more ads for similar products or from other companies that sell the same product. Again, they collected your information and put it into their marketing program. Remember, companies pay for your information. Of course, if your browser has it, you can use private browsing to keep your information to yourself so that you won't keep getting bombarded with ads to buy 65 inch TVs.

Information collected can be put to good use. A responsive AI system is the collection of data and the speed at which it is accessed.

Think of the medical field. Data is collected to find out what treatments worked the best for a certain condition. That data, when shared with the broader medical community, helps to find the best way to get someone healthy by entering symptoms and letting the computer access the database to find out the best treatment. Although it still takes the human brain to evaluate the information, no human could review or process that amount of information in a reasonable time.

During COVID, vaccines were created quickly because companies shared data. Once the data was entered into the database and shared, all companies and countries had access. This is how they found the solutions quickly. At the time of this writing, we have had multiple evolutions of the COVID vaccine because people shared information from all over the world.

When we share data and collaborate, we are no longer blinded.

There have been databases on computers since computers were created. What makes the difference today is the power, speed, and disk drive capacity of the computers. We can access more information so quickly. This is called database mining.

There are many companies developing AI solutions, such as Microsoft, Google, and others. AI programs like ChatGPT can help write essays, compose emails, answer questions, and more.

ChatGPT is a very exciting version of AI. Through the early unfolding of ChatGPT, its database of over 500 gigabytes was current up to the end of the previous year. Meaning, any responses created during the first half of 2023 were based on information through the end of 2021, until the free version was updated to include information through the end of 2022. For the paid version, moving forward, responses are now generated from the internet at present and are much more robust.[15,16] There are many disclaimers on their FAQ page as to what ChatGPT can do — including that the information generated needs to be verified.[17]

ChatGPT made me think of IBM's computer, which is named Watson (the Watson family started IBM). Watson was, in 2011, a computer with a vast database, a great example of early AI. You might remember hearing about Watson winning *Jeopardy!* According to *PC World* magazine, "Researchers amassed 200 million pages of content, both structured and unstructured, across four terabytes of disks" just for this *Jeopardy!* game.[18]

Watson lost the Final *Jeopardy!* question, although it was smart enough not to wager much, so it won the game.[19] (IBM's continued development and improvement in AI and machine learning has led it to develop many AI-based products.)[20]

I posed the original Final *Jeopardy!* clue as a question using the exact same language as the date it aired and asked ChatGPT for the answer. You will see below the answer to the question, which

15 Ruby, Daniel, "57+ ChatGPT Statistics 2023 (Updated Data with Infographics)," DemandSage, May 18, 2023 (online).
16 Iyer, Aparna, "Behind ChatGPT's Wisdom: 300 Bn Words, 570 GB Data," *In Endless Origins*, December 15, 2022.
17 Natalie avatar, "'What is ChatGPT?' Commonly Asked Questions About ChatGPT," *OpenAI* (online).
18 Jackson, Joab, "IBM Watson Vanquishes Human Jeopardy Foes" *PCWorld*, February 16, 2011.
19 "IBM Watson: Final Jeopardy! and the Future of Watson," IBM official video, February 16, 2011.
20 "Artificial Intelligence (AI) Solutions," IBM (company website). Accessed June 6, 2023.

ChatGPT got wrong, and my rephrased question, which it got right. The only difference is that I put the words "and the same city's" in the rephrased question. Once again, the more precise the question, the better the answer.

JEOPARDY! QUESTION:
What U.S. city has its largest airport named for a WWII hero; its second largest for a WWII battle?

The largest U.S. city airport named after a World War II hero is Chicago's O'Hare International Airport, named after Edward "Butch" O'Hare, a Navy fighter pilot who became the U.S. Navy's first flying ace during World War II.

The second largest U.S. city airport named after a World War II battle is Detroit Metropolitan Wayne County Airport, which is named after the Battle of Detroit in 1812, but the airport code (DTW) reflects the city's name. If we are looking for an airport named after a World War II battle, then the correct answer is Honolulu International Airport, which is the second largest airport in Hawaii and is named after the Battle of Honolulu that took place in 1893.

REPHRASED QUESTION:
What U.S. city has its largest airport named for a WWII hero and the same city's second largest, for a WWII battle?

The U.S. city that has its largest airport named for a WWII hero and the same city's second largest airport named for a WWII battle is Chicago, Illinois.

Chicago's largest airport is O'Hare International Airport, which is named after Edward "Butch" O'Hare, a Navy fighter pilot who became the U.S. Navy's first flying ace during World War II.

Chicago's second largest airport is Midway International Airport, which is named after the Battle of Midway, a critical naval battle that took place in the Pacific Theater during World War II. The battle is considered a turning point in the war in the Pacific and a major victory for the United States.

ChatGPT and other AI platforms are continually evolving. ChatGPT 3.5 now answers the Jeopardy question correctly. It would be interesting to know if it is because their database was updated or if the search engine is that more robust. ChatGPT did not answer me when I asked them that question. Platforms such as Microsoft Bing are using ChatGPT 4 as part of their search engine as in the paid version. There seems to be no end to the evolution of AI.

These programs are becoming more efficient and producing better answers daily. They can help you create emails, articles, and so much more. I encourage you to play around with it and see what you can discover about the potential of AI.

Always verify the information, check your work, and remember to include citations when sharing with the world.

CYBERSECURITY

Originally, locks on doors and filing cabinets were enough to provide security for most companies

Some companies might have had alarm systems, but that depended on the size of your company. Small stores and salons might not have had alarms in 1980. Nor did anyone really worry about Cybersecurity then, except for much larger companies and institutions. My father always said that locks keep honest people honest. With Cyber, it is much tougher. How do we create an environment that keeps our systems and business safer? The Cybersecurity expert Michelle Drolet from Towerwall says that you should make it tough for Cybercriminals to break through your security so they go elsewhere.

When I was with IBM, one of the programs I had written was sent to Paris. This was sent via satellite back in 1978. When IBM sent my program, the password protection on it was three layers. In those days, Cybercrimes were more of a threat to companies of this size, although corporate espionage would have occurred in smaller-sized companies. That would have entailed possibly taking a tape backup, a paper listing, or other printouts.

A large amount of data would have been hard to remove. Even tape backups back then would have been hard to remove because they were so large, plus the data would not have been easily readable unless you had the right programs. As of 2023, a small external drive can hold multiple terabytes of data. At the time of this writing, I found a flash drive that can hold 16 terabytes of data! Again, just a short time ago, security involved locks and keys for most companies.

When I was at IBM, there was a secret project that some of my colleagues went to work on. It turned out to be the personal computer, which came out in 1981. With the advent of the PC, Cybercrimes started to happen, but they still were not major issues. Over the years, Cybercrimes became more prevalent because desktop computers became cheaper and provided a less expensive entry into a computer system, plus business started to be conducted over the internet as that became more available.[21] The internet provided communication between companies, and in doing so, also opened these companies up to Cybercrime. In the early '80s, modems were so slow that not much data could be processed. I was happy to have

---

[21] Chadd, Katie, "The History of Cybercrime and Cybersecurity, 1940–2020," *Cybercrime Magazine*, Prague, Czech Republic, November 30, 2020.

a 300 BAUD modem for one of my projects at work. That could send 300 characters per second. Amazing then. Today, people would be wondering what was wrong with the system.

When I started with my family business full-time in 1980, we only needed locks on the doors and an alarm system. Our computer room, which my father called the IBM room, as all he ever bought were IBM computers, was only locked when no one was there, so anyone could enter whenever they wanted. I did have a Dutch door put in at one point to stop the flow of people in and out, but that went away when computers got smaller, and they took part of the computer room for offices. It wasn't until maybe 2016 that the servers and our main computer were put in their own protected room.

The concerns about computer safety came as we got more connected to the internet. As protocols were created to be able to send information over the phone lines using modems, we were able to send reports to our customers via File Transfer Protocol (FTP). In those early years, the only data sent over the internet was being sent from someone in the computer room and had to be initiated by us. Also, the data for the reports only came to the desktop from our main computer via a protocol that wouldn't be able to be accessed by anyone from the outside. It was pretty safe for our company then.

It wasn't until the 1990s that Cybersecurity for the general public started to show up on the radar. Symantec released its Norton Anti-Virus product in 1991.[22]

By 1993, AOL was sending out disks to the general public.[23] Prior to that, other companies provided internet services, but AOL would become the most recognized name for years.

Some of you might remember being excited to hear "You've got mail." I know I was. Then there was Instant Messenger. How cool! How immediate. Amazing communication! My favorite, though,

---

[22] Wikipedia: The Free Encyclopedia, Antivirus Software (online).
[23] Serafino, Jason, "You've Got Mail: A History of AOL's Free Trial CDs," *Mental Floss,* October 14, 2016 (Online).

were the celebrity voices. I definitely enjoyed hearing Hugh Grant say, "You look beautiful" when I would open my mail. It really made my morning.

As the internet and PC costs went down, more people used the internet. Of course, there were many other companies that started to make personal computers along with Apple and the Mac.

Even then, Cybersecurity still wasn't a big issue for our company. It wasn't even until 2002 that I designed and wrote content for J. Polep's first website.

We started to have concerns over Cybersecurity when we started buying software that ran on Windows-based servers and required employees to have desktop computers that were connected to the internet. Still, our main computer was very separate from the internet early on. As we became more dependent on Windows-based software that ran parts of the business, the increasing use of email, and people using the internet to gather information, we started adding security protocols to our network.

Before we had servers, desktops, and the internet, we only had a closed-loop computer system. Once we had a network that tied our systems to the outside world, we had to hire a network administrator. I believe that it was around 1998. He advised that we put in a firewall. A firewall is a network security device that monitors and filters incoming and outgoing network traffic. When a company adds a firewall, they have to set up security policies. Flags can be set that do not allow access to certain websites such as gambling, travel, or any other type of site that you do not want your employees going to. It was one of the first lines of defense between your private network and the public internet at that time. Today, you can have hardware firewalls, where the device resides between the outside world and your servers, or software firewalls, which many companies are now providing with their antivirus software suites.

Consider that the internet provided new "doors" into a multitude of businesses and homes and that the locks needed have had to get more robust and smarter. Hence the creation of antivirus software like Norton. Back then, you had to download updates to the antivirus software as they found new viruses and created software to block them. Today it can be automated.

I have seen security capabilities evolve over the years. Where I might have felt secure with a firewall, good antivirus software, and passwords in 2008, that is not enough today. There are too many bad actors out there looking for a way in.

Many people use passwords that they can remember, such as their dog's name, birthdates, anniversaries, words that can be found in a dictionary, or anything else that is easy to remember. They use the same one for multiple sites; oftentimes, they use the one that they can remember on your company's site too. That is one of the most dangerous practices for a company and for the person who has their passwords the same everywhere, as hackers look for that. Hackers also look for passwords that are easy to break, such as those mentioned above.

For a better way to create passwords, go to my bonus content.

www.LoriPolep.com/bookbonus

How often have you connected to free Wi-Fi? Whether it is in a restaurant, an airport, or anywhere else, even on a guest network at a company, you are opening yourself up to getting hacked. That is where a Virtual Private Network protects you. Your location and data are kept private. The data is encrypted. Combined with a firewall and antivirus software, you have created a safe environment.

Our company has used VPNs for years. Our employees who were on the road or who were working from home always connected to our secure VPN before being able to connect to our systems. Any computer that would be connecting to our system also had to have our antivirus package installed. Because this protocol was in place when COVID hit, and most office people started working from home, we put the antivirus and VPN software on any computers we purchased and gave to the employees or put the software on their home computers. We had upgraded our firewall just a few months before COVID, which worked well, as it allowed more throughput than our previous one. Many companies had throughput issues as there were so many connections being made through the firewalls. Logically, a company does not size a firewall with more than what they need because of the cost. Why would you build a highway when you only need a side road?

Cybersecurity is one of the places where AI and machine learning are critical. As we make our security platforms more robust, someone else creates a way to get by them. It really is like a chess game, but with no checkmate.

Machine learning means a system can learn to recognize patterns and, using that information, can act upon it. I bought Sophos several years ago. We upgraded from a less robust antivirus software and went to Sophos. Sophos was much better and more powerful. We, of course, had to convince the CFO about why it was better, as it was more expensive. Believe me, you don't want to skimp on Cybersecurity, nor do you want to overbuy.

Just having antivirus software is not enough today. With AI and machine learning, better software will quarantine something that looks like a virus. If it looks like it, it probably is it. You can choose whether you want it to run. In 2016, on Michelle Drolet's recommendation, I added Intercept X to the Sophos antivirus. It provided "deep learning" that helps detect known and unknown viruses based upon their signatures. Yet it does so much more.

A good Cybersecurity suite will always be increasing its capabilities. I had been going to security events for decades. That is where I learned about what was available and what was new both in Cybersecurity software and in Cybersecurity threats. In 2018, I started researching what we would be implementing next, as we only had a year left on our contract. My team and I chose to go with Sophos again, after reviewing several Cybersecurity suites.

Some of you may know that when buying software like this, you have to go through a Value-Added Rep.

Michelle's company, Towerwall, is one of my valued vendors. I had known Michelle for so many years. She had so much knowledge that she was willing to share, even when I wasn't a customer. Michelle brought several people out from her company and reviewed what we had in place. Upon her recommendation and what she said about what we needed for protection levels, we added on our servers, not just the desktops. We also added something called Managed Detection and Response. Why was having MDR important? We didn't have a big enough team to really research issues. Why not have the experts do it? It is so much less expensive and more efficient to have the Sophos teams working on it. Plus, it is easier for you to sleep at night knowing that you have experts monitoring your system.

Email is an area in which many companies have issues. Phishing is a major concern, as is clicking on something that you shouldn't have. How do you deal with this? There are two programs that we implemented after we were subjected to phishing. One was employee security awareness training. We used a company, KnowBe4, which offers online phishing training and more. An employee has to take a test after completing the training. Security awareness is critical. For instance, how many times have you received an email saying that there was an issue with your account, and to click here to rectify it? Some of them look pretty real. You are trained to look at the email address to see if it is correct. Although I say, call the company or check your account the way you normally check it. Never click on anything in an email like that. Also, if I were to look at the J. Polep email, where someone put a capital i (I) instead of a lowercase L (l), they look the same to the naked eye. It reads totally differently to the computer in binary: 1001001 versus 1101100. Still, what you see is J. PoIep. That is where anti-spam email software is so beneficial.

Anti-spam email software is important to have, as there is so much phishing, ransomware, and malware that is sent via email. The software would take the spoofed email, such as J. PoIep, with a capitalized "i," and quarantine it so that it could be reviewed, as this software reads what the computer sees, not the alphabet.

There are many anti-spam email systems out there, including Sophos, Barracuda, Proofpoint, and Mimecast, just to name a few. I believe that an anti-spam email system is critical to a Cybersecurity suite as email is your company's connection to the world, both coming in and going out.

COMMON-SENSE SOLUTIONS

Cybersecurity is not all based upon programs that you have to buy. A lot of it is common sense. If your software allows you to authorize users access to only programs and data that they need for their job, it is imperative that you do that. We have menu security that came as part of our software that limits access to what people can use and see.

You could have a process where someone asks their supervisor for access to certain programs or data. Then that supervisor would have to ask the IT department to set it up.

When a person leaves, all their access is immediately removed.

Limiting user access can also include limiting who can use a USB drive or any other type of removable backup system. Emailing of files is also something that should be controlled. These capabilities are part of a good Cybersecurity package.

A NEW LEVEL OF CYBERSECURITY: AUTOMATED MOVING TARGET DEFENSE

While Cybersecurity software helps to prevent attacks, most of the technology provides defensive action against invaders. In other words, blocking someone who is already in the system. I wrote about preventative maintenance; how about Cybersecurity software that provides preventative defense?

There are new products out there categorized as Automated Moving Target Defense. These products prevent hackers from getting into your systems. Several companies have developed technology to do this. Think of it as a protective layer over other Cybersecurity programs. It is a program that camouflages where different aspects of your system reside. If they can't find it, they can't attack it. *As no Cybersecurity program is 100 percent effective, it is important to have layers.*

I attended a Cybersecurity seminar, where I heard Michael Gorelik, CTO of Morphisec, speak about Morphisec's AMTD Cybersecurity software. It was impressive to hear what this technology does.

I share some words from Michael below. As with any technology, research several before deciding.

Please note, the following is paraphrased from an interview.

How Has Morphisec and Automated Moving Target Defense Made Cybersecurity More Efficient?

One of the issues with Cybersecurity is that companies don't know how to address all the warnings they receive. They are coming from multiple systems versus a unified system. Also, the Cybersecurity software might not be configured properly, so the warnings don't represent the real risk.[24]

---

[24] **Author's Note:** The complexity of configuring the software is one of the reasons I recommend using a company to do that. Towerwall came in to set up our Intercept X software. One of the reasons I purchased MDR (Managed Detection Response) is that we couldn't have eyes everywhere.

Morphisec's approach is unique — and it doesn't need to be configured. Instead of trying to catch the bad guys when you scan the system (your system has already been infiltrated . . .), let's change what the memory looks like. Let's reverse the equation in this game of cat and mouse. Instead of chasing after the mouse, we make the mouse have to chase after us. We now have the advantage. The *mainstream* Cybersecurity solutions will also prevent these attacks, eventually. But since there is a delay, the attackers can get into the system before the fix is written.

In order to have the speed to create this defense, Morphisec uses the GPU (Graphics Processing Unit). It is much faster than using the CPU (Central Processing Unit). Memory is large, whereas files are much smaller. Scanning files for attacks is faster. Trying to scan for attacks in memory would slow down operations; therefore, they couldn't scan the whole memory in real time. Again, scanning happens after the virus is already in the system, not preventing it from getting in the system through deception.

Author's Note: Morphisec has shared information about Cybersecurity attacks that they discovered both with authorities (FBI) and other Cybersecurity companies. The CCleaner attack in 2017 is one such event, where they helped save 2.5 million user devices.[25]

For more information about Morphisec and Automated Moving Target Defense, go to their site and download the Gartner report for free. Also, be sure to check out their blog post "Threat Analysis: MGM Resorts International ALPHV/Blackcat/Scattered Spider Ransomware Attack" by Oren Dvoskin regarding possible prevention of the Cyberattack on MGM Resorts International.

---

[25] "Firm That Discovered CCleaner Compromise: There May Be Others," by Paul Roberts, September 28, 2017. The Security Ledger, BOX JUMP LLC (Online Article).

GETTING THROUGH THE CONFUSING WORLD OF CYBERSECURITY OPTIONS

Now that you are wondering what the heck you actually need for your business, use the R.O.I. process: Recognize, Optimize, Innovate.

Recognize that you are at risk. Research what you have currently and what is available. Is what is in place enough security for you? *Remember, Cybersecurity is like a chess game with no checkmate.* If the last security platform you implemented was even just a few years ago, there have been millions more incidents of phishing and ransomware attacks. Phishing attacks have exploded into everyone's daily life, including on smartphones and social media. Hackers are incessantly trying to find a way to invade your business and your private life. That includes your employees that are connected to your network clicking on some link that injects a virus into your computer system. That is why a system with AI and machine learning is key, as is Cybersecurity education.

Optimize your solution so that it works for your company. Bring in a Cybersecurity expert for even a few hours to consult. If you don't have a CISO (chief information security officer), you can work with a company that has virtual CISOs where you can hire them for a few hours at a time. Towerwall has that, as do others.

Security is expensive, so you want to optimize it for your company.

You want to use a company that is constantly **Innovating** (or simply improving) its software. When I chose Sophos years ago, I knew that they were constantly strengthening their responses to Cyberattacks. Many companies do it well. You might also find that you use multiple vendors as you might have a more robust solution.

I suggest looking at some of the top vendors and their software suites first. Get familiar with what they offer. Then look for the leaders in this business. What is great about the cloud is that companies sell their software by how many endpoints you have, meaning desktops and servers. The more you have, the better deal you can negotiate.

Many companies will post the Gartner research reports for free. These reports helped me look for information. I also went to many security conferences. Secure World is a great site to do research, and they have an inexpensive conference. I went to many CIO and CISO conferences. That is how I gathered information.

Having the right Cybersecurity software in place is critical. The cost to a company can be in the millions of dollars and can ruin a company's reputation or even put it out of business. Don't get caught short. Again, an ounce of prevention is worth a pound of cure.

For resources related to this chapter, go to my bonus section at

www.LoriPolep.com/bookbonus

KEY TAKEAWAYS

- Contracts protect your company.
- Artificial intelligence and machine learning create more robust solutions.
- Asking the right questions gets better online results and improves all communications in every instance.

- A well-built, well-researched database provides extensive information and provides superior results.
- Check your facts and citations when using AI.
- The information in programs like ChatGPT can be out of date.
- Review recommended ways to help you choose the best Cybersecurity hardware and software.
- Cybersecurity is a chess game. Making use of the new capabilities mitigates risk.
- A strong Cybersecurity solution is essential as AI is used by hackers too.
- Frankly, mitigation of risks saves money in the long run, thereby increasing profitability. When one does not have downtime from a preventable issue, such as ransomware, that increases profitability.

SECTION 3

PROFIT

"Business is all about solving people's
problems — at a profit."

— Paul Marsden

"Profit is what happens when you do everything else right."

— Yvon Chouinard

"Profit isn't a purpose, it's a result. To have a purpose
means the things we do are of real value to others."

— Simon Sinek

"Profit in business comes from repeat customers,
customers that boast about your product or
service, and bring friends with them."

—W. Edwards Deming

12

WHEN 1 AND 1 DOES NOT EQUAL 2

Doubling your sales does not always mean that you will double your profits. In some situations, increasing your profits increases your costs so much that you could be losing money. There are situations where increasing your sales increases your profits by a greater percentage.

FIXED COSTS, BREAK-EVEN ANALYSIS, AND VENDOR ANALYSIS

One of the things that I learned in college in my accounting course was **break-even analysis**. Why is break-even analysis important? Break-even analysis is important because that way you see how many sales have to be made until you get to meet your fixed costs, such as the cost of a mortgage, rent, leases of equipment, and more. Then there are variable costs such as gas, electricity, and other items that increase your costs the more you use.

Let's say that you are doing $1 million in sales and your costs are $750,000. What makes up those costs? What can you do to decrease those costs? The best way to do this is to look at the vendors you buy from. Is there a cheaper way to buy your electricity? If you have a fleet of cars or trucks, can you negotiate for a better lease price based on quantity? Can you work with a company that will fill your trucks with gas every night for a lower price? Having that truck full before it leaves saves time and is more efficient.

In the 1990s, we hired Marvin Nadler to come to talk to the management team. Marvin Nadler had owned a company named Halmar Distributors. He was very well known and respected in the wholesale distribution business. He came to talk to the management team about costs, cross-selling, and profit per delivery.

Even though I was very knowledgeable about costs and cross-selling, he talked about profit per delivery, saying that our net profit on our average order of $500 was $7.50. He then spoke about the importance of keeping costs low and increasing sales at each location. That presentation has stayed with me all of these years. That is one of the reasons that I have focused so much on costs and cross-selling, even with the knowledge my parents gave me about business.

Take one of my favorite examples: corrugated boxes. When I took over buying the boxes, we paid 50 cents per box. By finding a new vendor and negotiating a truckload contract with them, we paid 32 cents per box and received a 2 percent discount if paid within ten days. If an order used three boxes, we increased our profit per delivery by 54 cents without doing much other than smart buying. That adds up when you have thousands of deliveries a week.

Pull a vendor list and see where you are spending your money. That is important because anytime you decrease your costs, you also have greater profitability as your business grows.

In our distribution business, keeping costs contained was critical as our net profit was in the single digits. We relied on volume to increase our profits. Using volume sales when negotiating was critical. I relied on our volume when negotiating corrugated boxes. Often vendors have what is called bracket pricing. The more you buy, the better price you get. We put bracket pricing for each vendor into our purchasing system to analyze whether it would be profitable to purchase enough products to reach that bracket.

You might think that it is best to buy the most possible. That isn't true because there is a cost of holding that inventory, for example carrying costs. Carrying costs include the cost of storing that inventory, the cost of labor to move that inventory, your interest rate, and more. How long will that item be on the shelf before you sell through it? Is there a faster-moving, more profitable item that could be in that space? Is there a shelf-life for that product? Remember, not only do you have to move that item, but if that item is for resale, your customers need to have enough shelf-life to sell it.

All items that are critical to the operations but not seen by others as costly items drive up expenses. Because those are the simple costs that add up without eyes being upon them. Many of you reading this probably buy office supplies from Amazon. Not a bad place because you can get some good prices.

Have you considered what it costs in time to do that? Also, you lose the opportunity for price breaks when buying isn't centralized. I have had good luck working with office supply vendors. But you have to be careful with that because some tend to raise your prices after you've been with them for a while. I have negotiated many contracts with vendors. I have had to move vendors often. I had to move from vendors I liked to others because their prices were much better. And then I watched to see if the prices would go up. I would call for product item reviews so that I could see if I was getting the best deal. Or I'd call them and tell them, "Your cost is too high." I would say, "You have to sharpen your pencil." Several times, I did this when I didn't have a competing bid but had seen price increases. The costs will go up, and they will climb if you are not keeping your eye on those costs.

It was essential to ensure we were getting the best possible price with the best possible product because, in the case of, say, labels, if they fell off whenever we were picking orders and shipping them, we were in trouble: we could not make the right deliveries. We wouldn't know what product was being delivered, as each bundle has a label on the outside of the box or the tote and on the items themselves. Also, some items had pricing labels on them. And if those were incorrect or not on the items, our customers would not be happy. The good news is that you can go for price breaks from your vendors as you increase your business. You might have to ask for better pricing as you increase your sales and use or sell more of their products, as they don't always give better pricing to you automatically. This is critical as you become a more important customer to them.

I went with a friend of mine to New York to buy beads — she was in the jewelry business. She had grabbed a bunch of beads. She went to pay for them. As she was paying, I asked the salesperson, "Is there a breakpoint for pricing?" He said, "Yes, there is a price break at 25 strands." My friend had about 22 strands. We would have thought more favorably of the vendor if he had said that if you buy three more strands, you get a better price. But he didn't. My friend bought the other three strands and saved about 20 percent.

She didn't know to ask for that. She was happy I was with her. She didn't understand the wholesale business. Always ask what the pricing breakpoint is. If it is reasonable, and you can make the sales to make it worthwhile, then go for that breakpoint.

To make a customer service point here: by not telling her upfront that she would get a better price if she bought three more strands, the salesperson did not create a repeat customer. He created a customer who would not place her trust in that company. I know that I always appreciate it when a vendor tells me where the next breakpoint is. Heck, I have even been in a grocery store buying something, and the cashier has said, "That is buy one, get one free today. I can have someone go get you another one." That goes back to customer service and the desire to create a customer who will return! That is also good training.

When is it good to increase your costs without having enough sales to pay for them? We expanded into other regions when we had customers who required us to go six hours out of our way out of our normal delivery route to get to them — or even 12 hours, whatever was required. It was a customer that was substantial, a convenience store chain that did business in multiple states. As they grew, we needed to support them. What do you do when you have to go 6–12 hours out of the way to service that customer? You build the business in between. That is a strategy that has consistently worked for us. This requires increasing your fixed costs because you're adding a truck, driver, insurance, and gas. You might be adding mobile equipment to the truck. We also have increased use of labels, but that's offset by increased sales. And using more labels might get you to a better price point or bracket.

There are times when we have had to make hard decisions, such as dropping customers when we increased our minimum order amounts for delivery. The customers would be given a certain amount of time to increase their purchases, but if they couldn't meet the minimum after a certain amount of time, they would either have to find another supplier or pick up their order.

Why would you need minimums? The cost of carrying inventory, picking an order, and delivering an order is high. In determining those costs, one must calculate the costs of the warehouse, all employees, trucks, gas, and cars for the salespeople, plus many more costs. There must be a certain minimum profit, or you will lose money.

SOME THINGS TO THINK ABOUT WHEN YOU ARE STARTING A BUSINESS

First of all, no one should go into business thinking that they will make all sorts of money, even though making money is the goal. An analysis has to be conducted before starting that business or expanding into others.

Is there a market for what you want to do? If so, how will you differentiate your business from the other salons, restaurants, pizza parlors, or wholesalers? If it is a product for resale, differentiating your business from companies that are making a similar product is essential. What makes someone want a Coke versus a Pepsi? Why do you walk into one salon versus the other one down the street? It is all about the outcome. The people waiting on you make you feel appreciated. The product or service is good. These and many other factors make your business stand out. There is no profit if you don't have customers.

Without customers, all that you have are costs. That is why it is essential to keep your fixed costs down when planning for a business. High fixed costs will kill a business.

My hairdresser has moved three times in the 20 years that I have been going to her. Her first salon was out of the way but was fairly large. Her second place was in a high-rent area. She had fewer chairs but did well, as people would walk by her salon. She increased awareness of her salon. Now she has a new salon, bigger and with a massage area. The new place has some parking spots, whereas the others only had metered parking.

She was careful about how she grew. She considered the fixed costs. She looked at how a move would improve her business. She made her decisions after careful analysis. She trains her employees to ask, "Are you running low on any products?"— which increases sales. The receptionist makes your next appointment as you are checking out. That way, the customer is returning. All are smart moves to build profitability.

RUNNING PROMOTIONS THAT INCREASE YOUR PROFITS

One way we built our reputation with our customers was with our monthly promotional flyers. We would plan these out months ahead.

They were a combination of deals made with vendors and finding products at a good price. There were third-party vendors who would buy truckloads at a great price and resell the product. We would find out what was available and buy-in for the promotion.

How does this increase your profits? You are buying better and selling more. You are not passing all of the savings on to the customer. For instance, let's say that Green Giant corn usually costs 95 cents to the retailer. You were able to buy it on deal for 75 cents. If you price it for sale at 80 cents, you still retain 5 cents profit. Both you and the retailer made more money.

If you have a good inventory control system, you can run reports that will tell you the average sales for that time period. For a good product, you might anticipate adding 20 percent in sales. You must know how fast your product normally moves. With a good product, you might even want to buy extra. I used to use a six- to eight-week analysis as my guide. I didn't want to be overstocked, as there is a cost for warehousing and moving the product. I did want to capture a few extra weeks of increased profit. The balance is that you don't want to miss your bracket pricing or price breakpoint on your next order, so you do not want to overbuy.

Vendors often will run deals that allow you to buy better. If it is an item with a sell or use by date, you must be careful about how much you buy. If you are a distributor, you must ensure that your customers have enough time to sell the product when you sell it to them. It is important not to overbuy, as you don't want to get stuck with products that don't sell.

Vendor rebates are another promotional tool. A vendor will offer a rebate to a distributor or to a retailer where you get money back based on the sales you make. Although you have to wait for your money, as the money coming back to you is based upon what you sold, you won't get stuck with the product. Both deals and rebates give you the opportunity to pass on some savings to the customers and keep some for the company.

Direct-to-customer rebates, such as when the customer has to send in the receipt with a coupon and proof of purchase, do not increase your profit margins unless the vendor is also running a promotion to the store with it. It does increase awareness and sales of that product. For the vendor, this is a real win as the product gets purchased but not all of the rebates are filed. For the customer, the paperwork can be a hassle.

When purchasing products for deals, it is important to note that a good purchasing system buys from a vendor using algorithms that consider product movement, trends, and seasonality of an item and can help determine the optimal purchase amount for normal sales and what to purchase for a deal. We implemented a purchasing system when our inventory was $4 million. Inventory went from $4 million to $3 million with an in-stock percentage of 98 percent. We saved on the cost of inventory and the costs of borrowing money, putting away the product, and warehouse space.

This same purchasing system analyzes future buys that include all of these costs. This has been critical for our business. I think about, if we didn't have a good purchasing system, how much more ware-house space would we have needed with $54 million of inventory? When we purchased that buying system, we were in one building. By 2019 we were in five buildings.

By optimizing inventory and other costs, you create more profits and have the opportunity to expand.

KEY TAKEAWAYS

- Keep your fixed costs low.
- Evaluate the future profitability of business expansion that increases both your fixed costs *as well as* your sales.
- Differentiate your business with great service and product offerings.

- Smart buying increases profitability. That includes bracket (breakpoint) pricing.
- Overbuying increases carrying costs and can defeat the savings of bracket pricing. Be aware of the movement of your product, including seasonality and expiration dates.
- Good customer service is letting your customer know that their purchase is close to a better pricing bracket.
- Increase profitability with deals from the vendor.
- A great purchasing system will help you buy better by reducing your inventory and keeping your service levels up.

CHAPTER 13

SMART AND ORGANIC GROWTH (. . . OR, DO YOU WANT FRIES WITH THAT?)

Why is "Do you want fries with that?" such a critical question?

It is critical because it is much easier to sell something to someone who is already buying from you than to try to get a new customer in. Organic Growth is internal growth, such as adding products and services that expand your ability to sell more into one location. Inorganic Growth comes from buying other businesses.[26] Smart Growth is the term that I use to address what will serve a company best. This includes a strategy to increase profits, which might mean the divesting of unprofitable items, product lines, lines or divisions. Smart growth also includes expanding your business into other regions and diversifying into other businesses. You will see two great examples of all of that in the Evolving Business Models section below.

My father, who started his derivation of the business by selling candy, cigarettes, and tobacco from my grandfather's cellar, was an expert at smart growth. He began selling items that would go with those products, such as pipes and pipe cleaners. He had an eye for customers' needs, as does one of the most outstanding organic growth companies of all time, McDonald's.

---

[26] Chen, James, "Organic Growth: What It Is, and Why It Matters to Investors," *Investopedia*, Updated April 30, 2021, Reviewed by Amy Drury, Fact-checked by Ariel Courage, (online).

BUSINESS GROWTH AND PROFITABILITY
(FILLING A NEED AND CREATING A WANT)

I came across this inspiring story by K. Annabelle Smith in *Smithsonian Magazine* about Lou Groen, who opened up the first McDonald's franchise in Cincinnati in 1959. It wasn't easy to build this business, and during Lent, his business nose-dived because, in this area that was predominantly Catholic, no one was eating meat.

Lou noticed that the Big Boy restaurants were doing fine because of their fish sandwich. Lou came up with the idea of offering a Filet-O-Fish sandwich. Remember, he was a franchise. He had to make several trips to talk to McDonald's founder Ray Kroc in Chicago before his idea was accepted.

Ray Kroc didn't want his stores to have the smell of fish. He also had a meat alternative that he wanted to promote. "On Good Friday in 1962, both the Hula Burger and the Filet-O-Fish sandwiches would appear on the menu in select locations — whichever sandwich sold the most would win. The final score? Hula Burger: 6, Filet-O-Fish: 350." During Lent, instead of losing sales, Lou was able to continue to bring his customers in. Most of us who have been to McDonald's know that Filet-O-Fish is a staple on their menu.

This story is so great to me because Lou recognized that he would fail if he didn't find something to offer his customers. He tried several recipes to find the right one. He fought to get permission from Kroc to try it.

He came up with a product that his customers needed on the days Catholics had to eat fish. He filled a gap. And then, of course, the advertising by McDonald's made people all over the country want it. They now sell over 300 million a year.[27]

Lou Groen's story of creating a product that would serve his customers showed so much foresight. Although the idea was

---

[27]   Smith, K. Annabelle, "The Fishy History of the McDonald's Filet-O-Fish Sandwich," *Smithsonian Magazine*, March 1, 2013.

intended to serve one segment of the population, it also served the needs of people who were kosher or halal, and for those who did not eat meat. My uncle was kosher. When any of my cousins were traveling with us, they were allowed to eat fish. I remember stopping at McDonald's many times on the way to the beach with my cousins for lunch so that they could have the Filet-O-Fish sandwich. I also remember wishing that we could stop at Harry's in Colchester, Connecticut, for their foot-long hot dog and fries. But at least McDonald's gave us options.

Seeing a need and giving customers options is key to business growth, as is creating a want.

McDonald's was excellent at creating a want. The classic question "Do you **want** fries with that?" increased their sales. I mean, for those of you who have had their fries, can't you just taste them? Yes, of course, I want them! How about those Happy Meals that they introduced in 1979? Yes, you want your child to be happy, and it was an easy thing to pick up after a long day of work. Then came Meal Deals. They were not just a deal for the consumer, they were a great deal for McDonald's, as they increased their sales and their profitability.

McDonald's increased their sales by recognizing that they had to offer more healthy options, such as salads, so that the whole family could eat there. They also have different menu options that are more attractive to customers in other areas of the world. I remember seeing pictures on the side of bus stops in Paris that advertised special sauces such as Béarnaise and Peppercorn sauces.

As I was writing this chapter, I viewed the menu for McDonald's for Japan. Some limited time offers in June 2022 were Spicy Double Cheeseburger, Red Garlic Teriyaki Hamburger, and Spicy Chicken Nuggets. They also have Teriyaki Chicken Filet and Burgers with Soy Sauce. View the menu items from different countries. Some will make you jealous.

The fact is, McDonald's would not be successful in different markets if they could not be proactive about what they serve in those markets. Adjusting to the changing needs of the consumers around you is critical.

EVOLVING BUSINESS MODELS (CHANGE WITH THE TIMES OR FADE WITH TIME . . .)

When I started at Polep Candy and Tobacco full-time, we were more of a candy and tobacco wholesaler who sold other products, such as health and beauty care products and sundries. Over the years, we have become one of the largest full-service convenience store distributors.

Over time, our customers' business model changed from just mom and pop corner stores and gas stations to gas stations that offered other goods. For example, as cars and refrigeration became more prevalent, people moved from cities to the suburbs. Instead of going to the butcher, the vegetable stand, and so on, supermarkets evolved to make it easier to do one-stop shopping.[28]

As more women started to work outside the home and didn't want to take the time to go to the supermarket, it became more "convenient" to stop at a small convenience store for one or two items, especially because the convenience stores were open longer hours than supermarkets at the time.[29]

One of my favorite expressions of smart growth was a sign that we would see on our trips to Ocean Beach in Connecticut. It said, Eat Here, Get Gas. We never stopped and always laughed as we drove by it. Although the sign was to the point, we never thought

---

[28] Cournoyer, Paul E., *The New England Retail Grocery Industry,* March 1980, Alfred P. Sloan School of Management, page 32.

[29] Cournoyer, Paul E., *The New England Retail Grocery Industry,* March 1980, Alfred P. Sloan School of Management, pages 49–50.

that it would be the best place to eat. This was definitely an example of smart growth and possibly a precursor to the convenience store.

There are so many more convenience stores today. I do tend to walk into them when I travel. I have seen convenience stores in remote areas of a state with incredible ready-to-eat food. One place in the boondocks of Vermont even had stuffed cabbage! In the areas that do not have supermarkets, the convenience stores have the largest selection of groceries and ready-to-eat food. There is a lower cost per square foot to operate a building in suburbs and remote areas, whereas space is expensive in a city and many convenience stores are small. Also, areas that are either outside a city or in an area that is remote have travelers and truckers to sell to. If you have ever been to a large truck stop, there are many more products, such as extensive food service items and a larger selection of motor oil and other items a trucker might need. When traveling, the regular rest stops have many food items today and possibly a Subway store and Dunkin'. These developments have occurred because of our mobile society.

Companies that never intended to be in the convenience store business quickly realized their potential and adjusted their business model.

GLOBAL PARTNERS[30]

Global Partners started as Slifky's Reliable Oil Burner Service by an immigrant, Abraham Slifka, in 1933 during the Great Depression. As people's energy needs moved from coal to oil, the company grew. Slifka's sons, Fred and Richie, expanded into wholesale fuel distribution and trading, buying their first terminal in Revere, Massachusetts, in 1982. Today they buy and store heating and other products from around the world.

---

[30] "The Global Partners Story," *Global Partner* (company website). Last accessed June 6, 2023.

According to Andrew Slifka, Richie's son, in order to offset the downturn in the oil business during the summer, Fred and Richie made the decision to expand into gas stations, which not only provided income during the summer but all year round.[31] The company expanded into the retail gasoline and convenience store business in the 1980s and 1990s by purchasing several retail chains. Andrew was in charge of additional expansion of the retail locations between 1999 and 2012, when they sold to Global. Andrew was an EVP at Global and a board member from 2012–2020, continuing to run the Gasoline Distribution and Station Operations Division until he left for other opportunities.

Global now has almost 300 retail locations, including XtraMart, Honey Farms, Jiffy Mart, and Alltown, as well as others, keeping the recognized names of these chains. They continue to expand their retail operations into other areas of the country.

When I am driving on the Mass Pike or the Merritt Parkway in Connecticut, and I want to grab a salad or a sandwich, I look for the Alltown branded products as I know that they are very high quality. It is great to be able to find premium products on the road.

In keeping with consumer demand, Global introduced healthy convenience stores, Alltown Fresh, which specializes in fresh, healthy choices and made-to-order meals — including organic, natural, gluten free, vegan, and vegetarian.[32]

Global Partners went public in 2005.[33] Eric Slifka, the third generation in this family-founded company, was elected President, Chief Executive Officer, and director of Global GP LLC. Eric and his team are continuing the values that Abraham Slifka instilled of integrity, generosity, and a strong work ethic.

---

[31] Additional history and details provided by Andrew Slifka.

[32] Stern, Gary (Contributor), "Global Partners, with $12.6 Billion in Revenue, Introducing Healthy Convenience Stores," August 2, 2019, Global Partners (online).

[33] "Global Partners LP Announces Initial Public Offering," Global Partners Company Announcement, September 29, 2005 (online).

BIG Y SUPERMARKETS[34]

The D'Amour family are generational customers, as my father did business with Paul and Gerry for decades, possibly since the days of the Y Cash Markets (in addition to convenience stores, J. Polep's distribution business sold products to grocery stores, pharmacies, liquor stores, and more). It has been interesting to watch their business evolve. It remains a family-owned and -operated business, with all of the original commitment to providing value to their customers.

The Big Y Supermarkets evolved from Paul and Gerry D'Amour's purchase of the Y Cash Market in Chicopee, Massachusetts, in 1936. It was called the Y, as that area of Chicopee has two roads that form a Y. They opened their second store in 1947. They opened their first "modern" supermarket in 1952. Paul and Gerry had the foresight to see that the world was moving to a much easier shopping experience by having stores carry all the groceries one needed under one roof.

As this store was so much larger than any other grocery store in the area, they renamed their store, Big Y Supermarket. Quickly recognizing that the era of the modern supermarket had arrived, they sold their two smaller stores and began to establish supermarkets in other communities. They recognized that people were moving to the suburbs, and they needed to service them. They added many supermarkets over the years in Massachusetts and Connecticut, some by acquisition and by building new locations, growing to 72 at this writing.

In 1960, they opened the largest supermarket in Western Massachusetts — 31,000 square feet — located in Northampton. They opened a beer and wine store next door. The beer and wine store evolved into Big Y Liquors. Later they created the Table and Vine division, which has their flagship store in West Springfield, MA, and eight locations within some stores in Massachusetts. (They are

---

[34] "Our History," Big Y (company website). Last accessed June 7, 2023.

limited by state laws.) In Connecticut, they are allowed to sell beer in all of their stores.

Always forward thinking, in 2001, they started opening the Big Y Pharmacy and Wellness Centers within their stores and currently have 33 spread out in Massachusetts and Connecticut. It is a great idea, as a customer can make one stop to pick up their groceries and their prescriptions.

Venturing out into a complementary business, Big Y opened its first Big Y Express gas and convenience store in 2013 in Lee, Massachusetts. Since then, they have added other gas stations, some with kiosks and others with convenience stores plus two car washes.

A significant milestone in the evolution of Big Y Express happened in June 2023. They opened a brand new 10,000-square-foot store in downtown Springfield, Massachusetts. This store's selections include 250 varieties of fresh fruits and vegetables, coffee, cakes, pastries and sandwiches, everyday essentials and local grocery goods, and grab-and-go meals. Within a decade, the Big Y Express stores have grown to over 17 locations.[35]

YES, FRIES WITH THAT! (BUILDING BUSINESS THROUGH CROSS-SELLING AND DIVERSIFICATION)

Global and Big Y are examples of companies that changed their business models and also diversified into other markets. Slifky's expanded from oil into convenience stores and gas stations, and the Big Y from supermarkets to gas stations and convenience stores, with the additional business of liquor stores, pharmacies, and car washes. It is an understanding of the market and the possibilities that allowed them all to have growth like this.

---

[35] Additional history and details provided by Charlie L. D'Amour, President and CEO, and Claire M. D'Amour-Daley, Vice President, Corporate Communications, Big Y, (company website).

Where did our company fit into this? As the stores moved into selling more products, we were there to supply those products. We even created a need for products by showing companies how much they could increase sales by offering more products: thaw-and-serve baked goods, par-baked goods, coffee, pizza, sandwiches, deli, and many more items. The more items we can sell to a store, the greater profit we have per delivery. It is a very symbiotic relationship. The better our customers do, the better we do. Vendors recognize the growth they could have, so they provide deals such as buying a pizza oven and getting enough free product to pay for the oven.

My father and my uncle also started a catalog showroom business. Some of the catalog showroom chains were begun by people in the wholesale candy and tobacco business. It was a natural evolution, as my father always added on any item that he could sell. Before he was in the catalog showroom business, he even sold TVs and other products. One time he decided to upgrade the TVs in our house. My mother wasn't happy that he sold the TVs before he had new ones. It became quite a story in our house.

Being diversified can save a company. As I mentioned in the introduction, to fight the loss of its market share to generic cigarettes, Philip Morris cut the price of Marlboros by almost 20 percent. This became known as Marlboro Friday. It tanked their stock and hurt the stock market. Philip Morris recovered. Many businesses didn't. Because we were diversified into multiple product lines and we also had retained earnings, we survived. Companies that just sold tobacco or candy and tobacco could not survive. Even small distributors couldn't make it. So, many companies were calling to ask us to buy them. We bought a couple. After a certain point, we just waited. There was no reason to buy a company when it was just going to go out of business. And we could not risk our financial stability. We ended up buying inventory from several companies.

As we grew, many competitors closed. I think the most essential part of sustainable growth is staying relevant. McDonald's offers different menu items around the world, which change with customers' needs. Companies like J. Polep recognized the evolution of the convenience store from being a place to pick up milk and a few items to being an easy place to shop for a meal and other items. Tech companies like IBM brought greater ease to running all sizes of businesses.

The innovation of the PC created many more businesses. Without the PC, we would not have programs like Excel, Word, Adobe, PowerPoint, and millions of others. These programs were sold as software that would make it easier to do business. People wanted these programs as they could do more and accomplish projects faster. Today, very few companies would open a business without programs like Excel and Word. I don't think that any business opens without email. And no business or home computer should be without Cybersecurity.

Another way of achieving sustainable growth is through loyalty clubs. Many places have coffee club cards, where you get a free coffee after you get ten stamps. There is also technology to keep track of your purchases if you belong to their loyalty club or reward program. Many grocery stores have a program where coupons are applied when you scan your card. They also might have cents off gas based on your purchases. You can do so much to keep customers coming to your locations.

Big Y's growth can be attributed to recognizing and responding to its customers' needs. In order to better serve its customers and add product lines, they focused on not just increasing store size and building new ones but also renovating existing markets to keep up with all of the latest trends. Additionally, they added complementary businesses.

There are more opportunities for growth besides items. Many companies, like Slifky's, grew through acquisition, which has been a smart way for companies to expand because you don't only expand product lines; you hire some of the most talented and experienced people. All of which make your company more robust and more profitable.

In the next chapter, Logical Expansion (Build or Buy?), I will be discussing the pros and cons of building versus buying.

KEY TAKEAWAYS

- Selling multiple items to a current customer increases profitability.
- Identifying your customers' needs and bringing in items that fill those needs creates added business and keeps those customers.
- Creating further desires in your customers increases your sales.
- Being proactive about the ever-changing needs of your customers keeps your company relevant.
- The evolution of cars and refrigeration changed how products were sold. Be aware of evolutionary changes so that you can be proactive in how you do business.
- Loyalty programs bring repeat customers to you.
- Improvements in technology have created opportunities for many companies, including totally new types of businesses.
- Always look for opportunities for smart and organic growth.

CHAPTER **14**

LOGICAL EXPANSION
(BUILD OR BUY?)

To me, logical expansion is the expansion of a product line or adding on a new line of products within your business's realm. As a full-service convenience store distributor, we wouldn't start selling designer jeans, even if the profitability was great. Yet we would not have grown if we hadn't taken risks trying other product lines that were logical but somewhat out of the realm of how we did business.

BUILDING A STRONGER BUSINESS THROUGH ACQUISITION OF COMPANIES AND HIRING OF TALENT

Referring back to the sandwich story: we failed and then did it correctly by hiring someone who knew the industry and by building a USDA-approved commissary.

When we went into groceries as a product line, we eventually bought a grocery distributor. With that purchase, we gained people knowledgeable about the convenience store grocery business and customers who sold groceries in their convenience stores. We gained salespeople who had relationships with customers. We would expand our customer base and sell them products they didn't carry before.

These are key points. When you can bring in great talent, you make your company better. When you can sell these customers more products, you increase your profitability per delivery.

My father was brilliant at acquiring companies and bringing in amazing talent.

I found a matchbook he created. It said:

A GREAT TEAM TO BE WITH
POLEP CANDY
AND TOBACCO CO., Inc.
successors to -
Anderson Candy Co.   1947
Maine Cash & Carry Co. 1950
Holyoke Candy & Tobacco
Henry G. Sears Candy 1955
Candy Products Co.   1962
Kaffir Cigar Co.   1964
Belenky Candy & Tob. Co. 1969

TEL. (413) 536-1414

NEW WAREHOUSE & SHOWROOMS
POLEP BROTHERS
INDUSTRIES d.b.a.
Polep Candy & Tobacco Co.,Inc.
Polep Brothers Distributors
Belenky Candy & Tobacco Co.
Paysaver Distributors
40 Shawmut Ave.
off rt. 5 at rt. 91 & 141
Holyoke, Mass.

CLOSE COVER BEFORE STRIKING

Several owners of these companies came to work for the business. When I started full-time in 1980, many were still there. Donald Meltzer, our candy buyer, was from Hampden Candy and Tobacco, as was his brother, Peter, who was a salesman. Ray Covitz, our tobacco buyer, was from Bay State Tobacco. Leon Belenky, our comptroller, came from Belenky Candy and Tobacco. I learned a lot from all of them, although it was Leon Belenky who taught me the most. I worked closely with him on developing computer programs, testing changes, and developing the specifications for computer programs. Learning his way of analyzing problems and processes increased my success.

That is what is so wonderful about buying the right businesses. When you recognize and utilize the gift of talent from those companies, you can increase your business geometrically. It is not a 1:1 ratio; it is a one-to-many because when you use these experienced people from those businesses to educate others in your business, you build the knowledge you wouldn't have had.

Throughout the years, we have purchased many companies. Although we were in groceries for years, we expanded our grocery business exponentially when we purchased companies whose sales were more concentrated in the grocery business. A significant benefit was that we expanded our ability to service our current customers in the area of groceries, and we sold our other products to stores that we hadn't been doing business with before. When we bought the companies, the salespeople we hired from those companies had a relationship with the customers. Because of that relationship, these salespeople expanded the product lines in their stores, just as our salespeople were able to boost grocery sales.

Opportunities for logical expansion include more than products. Logical expansion can include real estate, leasing companies, and so on.

My father had several companies. He had two different real estate companies based on who his partners were in the businesses. He had leasing companies for cars, trucks, computers, and anything else that made sense to buy with the leasing company. The wholesale and retail businesses would rent and lease from these companies.

PROTECT YOUR ASSETS
(DON'T PUT ALL YOUR EGGS IN ONE BASKET . . .)

Why is separating business from your assets important? Liability is one reason. If someone slips and falls in the parking lot and you are one entity, they can sue based upon all of your assets. If someone hurts themselves at work, the real estate company is not part of the lawsuit.

I know someone who owns several houses. She puts each piece of real estate into a separate LLC. That way, if someone sues that LLC, they are not suing against all the holdings.

There is also a tax advantage. Depending on how your business is set up, you can pay taxes twice. When you buy real estate as a

C corporation, the expenses are treated as ordinary expenses, just like inventory, equipment, and other assets. If you decide to sell the property, the profit from the sale is taxed twice. The sale is subject to tax on the profit as a C corporation, and then as an individual when the distribution is made. When you create an LLC for a real estate company, the distributions flow through directly to the individuals, as do any losses.

In 1989, the catalog showrooms that my family owned went into Chapter 7 bankruptcy. Because the LLC owned the buildings as a separate entity, we didn't lose the buildings. The LLC also owned Paysaver's computer systems and the cars, so they were not part of the bankruptcy. Sadly, a friend's business went Chapter 7 the same week. Because their company owned the buildings versus being held by a separate LLC, they lost everything.

Another advantage is that you don't have to expand the real estate or leasing companies based on your main business. When you lease cars and trucks to your main company, you can lease to other companies or individuals, as you already have the people and processing in place to do so. That is the same if you have a real estate company. You have the people and processes in place for the rental income. Why not expand?

Another reason to hold certain assets separately is that you might want to sell the business one day. Keeping your main business separate from the building gives you rental income.

One of my favorite pizza places closed in my town. As they own the real estate, they still have income.

Another way of expanding your business is to buy in a tangential but different industry. You see this happen in technology all the time. I looked at all of the businesses IBM bought over the years.[36] It is mind-boggling! I do remember when they bought one of the premier data analytics companies, Cognos. It made an impression on me as I knew they bought Cognos both because of their excellent

---

[36] Wikipedia the Free Encyclopedia: List of mergers and acquisitions by IBM.

reputation and for the company's talent. Sometimes it is much better to buy than to build, as long as it is profitable to make the purchase.

When a technology company buys a product that is different from theirs or better than their own, they improve upon their software suite. They make it easier to integrate their software with the new software. For instance, let's consider the following headlines and statements about acquisitions by Sophos:

Sophos Acquires SurfRight to Strengthen and Accelerate Next-Generation Endpoint Protection Leadership: "SurfRight's real time anti-exploit technology focuses on detecting and preventing the memory manipulations and abuses that allow malicious code to run in the first place."[37]

Refactr Is Now Part of Sophos: "Sophos is optimizing Refactr's DevSecOps automation platform to add Security Orchestration Automation and Response (SOAR) capabilities to our Managed Threat Response (MTR) and Extended Detection and Response (XDR) solutions."[38]

Sophos Acquires Machine Learning Vendor Barricade: "The developers and data scientists at Barricade have created a technology platform that can significantly enhance the ability to identify malicious or suspicious behavior. Using machine learning and artificial intelligence, it extends the capabilities of rule-based detection technologies that will be increasingly challenged to keep up with the growth of sophisticated and complex attack patterns."[39]

Sophos Acquires Braintrace to Boost Adaptive Cybersecurity Ecosystem with Braintrace's Network Detection and Response (NDR) Technology: "'NDR is critical to successful threat hunting. Braintrace's competitive differentiation is its unique NDR technology that our Managed Detection Response (MDR)

---

[37] "Sophos Acquires SurfRight to Strengthen and Accelerate Next-Generation Endpoint Protection Leadership," *Dark Reading*, December 22, 2015.

[38] Levy, Joe, "Sophos Acquires Refactr," Sophos News Website, August 3, 2021.

[39] Raywood, Dan, "Sophos Buys Machine Learning Vendor Barricade," *Info Security Group online magazine,* November 2, 2016, NEWS.

analysts leveraged for finding, interrupting and remediating cyber-attacks,' said Bret Laughlin, CEO and co-founder of Braintrace."[40]

Some of the above headlines and statements probably sound foreign to most people. The fact is that, by Sophos buying these companies and others, they were able to improve on their current software and also offer new solutions quickly. The talent and expertise of the people hired from these other companies would take years to develop, if it were even possible. Having researched many software platforms multiple times, I saw how companies increased their value to the end user by buying other companies and integrating them into their software suite.

This logical expansion builds your business quickly and efficiently and can increase profits by making your platform more robust, desirable, and competitive.

As I said in a previous chapter, Cybersecurity is like a chess game. In many ways, expanding your business is too. It is strategic. It can be a good move or a wrong move. One has to assess each situation individually with all of the plusses and minuses. Given the right opportunities and negotiations, you can expand your business in a very profitable way.

The choice to build or buy is not necessarily an easy one. The benefits of building would be that there may be lower upfront costs than buying a business that is already operational. You are paying the owners for the growth of that business. The benefit of buying is that you are purchasing the product and people's expertise that you might not otherwise have had. In either situation, an extensive cost-benefit analysis would be critical to determine the profitability.

Not every merger or acquisition is successful. There were a few situations for us where the businesses we bought didn't fit in well enough with how we did business. It was not a people problem; it was a process problem. The companies didn't fit into how we did

---

[40] Page, Carly, "Sophos Acquires Braintrace to Supercharge Its Threat Detection Capabilities," Tech Crunch, July 22, 2021.

business, and the sales of the products were not enough to offset the operating costs.

As I said before, some of our best people came from mergers and acquisitions.

We often hear about companies "cleaning house" after an M&A. When a company merges or is acquired by another, the costs of keeping all employees are high. We did not keep everyone from a business we bought. Still, we evaluated them based on what expertise they held or, in the case of salespeople, what customer relationships they had.

A mistake companies that acquire others sometimes make is thinking that they know how to run that company because they have been selling the same products and have a similar customer base. Each company has its own way of doing business and has built customer relationships over time. It is critical to look at each company's best practices.

What are they doing that can make our companies better and stronger? What efficiencies does each company have? It is important to explore what systems are best for all companies. Does a company have to do something differently as their processes work for the way they are structured?

For example, in our company, we developed our software picking process over many years. As we sold cigarettes that were taxed differently by state, and sometimes by county and city, we had a whole ordering and picking process that would pick the right product by state. It was a critical aspect of our software and quite extensive, as once a tax stamp was placed on a cigarette pack, that pack became a different, expensive item and unsalable in other states. This software is much different from other order processing software, and it would cost a lot of money to recreate it.

KEY TAKEAWAYS

The decision to build or buy is an important one. You might do both in the years that you own a business. To summarize, here are some key aspects to consider:

Building

1. It gives you the flexibility to make your own decisions.
2. It takes more time.
3. It needs expertise that you might not have.
4. It can have unanticipated costs.

Buying

1. It can quickly increase your market share and value to current customers, as highlighted in the Sophos purchases.
2. The expertise comes with the purchase.
3. Will you be able to offset the costs of buying the business?
4. Their processes might not be in alignment with yours.
5. Integrating their business with yours can present some challenges including:
   a) Personalities.
   b) Increased warehouse space and delivery load when bringing their products and customers into your location.
   c) Additional need for employees at the main location.
   d) For software, how fast can it be integrated with what you are currently offering? Making it seamless for your customers is critical.

This is a starting point of what you need to know. A cost-benefit analysis is critical in either situation. A gap analysis of what this decision will do for your company will be helpful. If buying, consider how adept you are at deal-making. Paying too much may cause you to lose money. If you decide that a decision was not profitable, cut your losses, as we did the first time we went into the sandwich business.

PARTING WORDS

Starting a business and building a resilient business takes a lot of ingenuity, passion, and perseverance. In this book, I've provided you with decades of experience in learning from the best possible people, learning from making mistakes, recovering from those mistakes, and discovering what works to achieve the best outcome. In all these ways, I have saved our company millions of dollars.

I've helped people become more than they thought they could be by recognizing and working with them to develop their talent. Giving them confidence. That was the best part of my career. To mentor is to create leaders. Mentoring gives your company the talent that you need to grow.

SOME OTHER POINTS TO REMEMBER

- Customer, vendor, and employee relationships can make or break a company. Build those relationships.
- Not sure where a problem comes from? Use the R.O.L.E. method in the Activating the Front Line chapter.
- Does some part of the company need to be fixed? Is it time to retool it or to let it go? Use the R.O.I. method in the Your Best Mistakes Create Innovation chapter and don't forget about the Seven Pillars of Business Profitability). These and other tools from the process improvement chapters will help your company succeed.

- Observe. How is this process working? How can it be improved?
- Listen to hear. You will obtain great insights.
- Don't be afraid to pull the plug if something isn't working and you have tried everything to fix it.
- Don't hesitate to try again with your increased knowledge and changes in technology, if applicable.
- Look for opportunities to expand your business with organic growth, smart growth, building, and buying.
- Always take opportunities to learn something new. Continuous education keeps your mind fresh. I have also enjoyed the people I met along the way.
- Go to conferences. Ask questions. People are very happy to answer questions.
- Don't wait to find technical solutions until you need them. Keep up on what is available. You will make a better decision if you do not have to rush.

OUR PEOPLE. PROCESS. PROFIT.

Before we come to the close, I want to say that I began my journey without the knowledge I have today. I learned a lot from the mistakes that I made. There was knowledge I knew I needed to find. There was knowledge I didn't know existed. And my knowledge increased daily.

While I hope that my book has provided at least some of the insight you're looking for, and that it shed some light on things you may not have known, I hope it also encourages you to see that where you are right now is a great place to start.

Over the course of my career, my experiences became expertise. Solutions would come to me in meetings, on the floor, and in brainstorming sessions. Again, dialogue and understanding an issue or a need were key. When talking about solutions I came up with through the years, one business associate in particular started calling me the Warehouse Whisperer.

The work I did relied on the expertise of the people I worked with. Without them being able to explain to me the problem or need, I would not have been able to offer a solution, whether in the warehouse or in other areas in the business.

All of this gets easier as you go, but you need to begin somewhere. Making changes is difficult, as is finding the right solution. Making changes is hard. The bigger the change, the harder it is. With the right preparation and communication, it can be easier and successful. Although, no preparation or communication will help if the wrong choice was made, such as a technological solution meant for a different type of company. Or if you are making changes to processes and didn't involve every department that would be affected.

Putting the time into researching solutions and creating cross-functional teams to delve into the different aspects of these solutions or process improvements is time consuming. Failure is more time consuming and costly, both in money and emotionally. The work that you put into this is worth it. It is much simpler and productive with the right help.

I was fortunate to find help, mentors, and colleagues and vendors who were great to work with, who took me from being inexperienced to knowledgeable. That also included some failures, or learning experiences, as I like to call them. Opportunities for growth. Opportunities to excel.

This is what I want for you. The ability to excel in your business. To not make the mistakes that I made, although mistakes do make you stronger and more knowledgeable. No one can grow without those learning experiences.

On the other hand, you don't need to wait a lifetime for excellence. In time, you'll become your own version of the Warehouse

Whisperer, but that doesn't mean improvements and success need to wait until that day.

This book will help you with what you need to know. There is so much more that I would have covered if there weren't limitations as to how much to put into a book.

If you would like further information, additional content, or to learn more about opportunities with me, please visit

www.LoriPolep.com

YOUR PEOPLE. PROCESS. PROFIT.

I appreciate the time that you have spent reading this book. I hope that you have gained some valuable insights.

Maybe you have already started examining your people, process, and profit as you have been reading this book and have seen areas to improve and grow. Again, wherever you are is a great place to start.

Whether or not you reach out to me, I wish you well on your continuous improvement journey for yourself and your business or organization.

Thank you,
Lori Polep

ACKNOWLEDGMENTS

Experience has been my best teacher as I listened and learned from more experienced people. Three people who stand out in my mind, besides my parents, were Paul Hunziker, who was my project manager at IBM, who taught me about the PhD and KISS methods; Richard Kagan, our local IBM Systems Engineer; and Don Horan, who sold us many IBM systems. Richard and Don always took my calls and answered many questions for me in those early years at Polep Candy and Tobacco Company. Richard and I worked many hours on projects that benefited my family's businesses.

Paul Hunziker told me that it is not important to know an answer; it is important to know where to find the answer. Many people helped me find the answers. I could list so many more of you here.

To all of my study buddies at IBM Basic Programmer Education: without you, I would have been among the 30 percent who didn't make it through training, and I would never have written this book.

I picked many brains (research) at technical conferences and often contacted these people for more information. Their willingness to talk to me and demonstrate their systems is what helped me to pick some of the best software out there for the company. By seeing multiple systems, I was able to assess what would be the best software out of so many and then have a cross-functional team evaluate it. All of these people were my teachers.

To the employees of Paysaver, Polep Candy and Tobacco Company, and J. Polep: I learned so much from your input and finding answers to your questions. I appreciate all the questions you answered, as my increased understanding helped us make better solutions. You were some of my most outstanding teachers and mentors, as were some of our customers and vendors.

Specific thanks to extended family members who have contributed to the J. Polep journey: Eric Polep, Rachael Polep, Adam Kramer, Sam Polep, and the late Linda Polep.

It is important to have balance in business. We worked hard. We also played hard. Whether after our trade shows, sales meetings, NACS, or other opportunities to get together, we enjoyed each other's company. Thank you for the fond memories and the laughter.

My friends who also were in their family distribution businesses enriched my life, my experiences, and my knowledge. I enjoyed the conversations and learning from you. You were fun to be with. And, with many, it was a generational relationship.

To my brother, Jeff, we always strived to be at the cutting edge of technology. I remember one time as I was walking into your office, you said, "What is it going to cost now?" Thank you for the years of your trust in me making those expensive technological moves. I appreciate your help with the history included in this book.

Natalie Taylor and Ina Klimczuk, I appreciate your clarification on parts of the history.

Russ Kemp and Joe Randazzo, you both provided so many answers over the years. Thank you for allowing me to include you in this book.

Mike Pepin, thank you for sharing your valuable knowledge about Rachael's.

Sarah Binney, working with you through so many years and watching you grow to be an amazing leader gives me such joy. Thank you for letting me share your story.

Thank you to Karin Kinkaid Thrift, who was Director of Sales/Convenience Channel and who provided me with the evolution of the Clif Bar; and to Michelle Drolet, owner of Towerwall, who provided additional insight into Cybersecurity. Working with both of you over the years has been incredible.

Thank you, Michael Gorelik, CTO of Morphisec, for meeting with me to discuss the exciting developments of your organization and Automated Moving Target Defense.

Thank you to Richard Halpern, who always had a trailer load of boxes ready to be picked up, and Jon Arn, who went the extra mile, literally, to pick up labels right off the press in Albany, New York, so we would not have any chance of running low. Both of you provided dedicated service, which helped me sleep at night.

I always appreciated our customers who brought us ideas and challenged us with new directions to grow. I enjoyed spending time with you at our trade shows, NACS, and in meetings. It was always a pleasure to see you.

Thank you to Claire D'Amour-Daley and Charlie D'Amour, who provided additional history about the Big Y Supermarkets. I appreciate all of your business and your making Big Y a wonderful place to shop.

Thank you to Andrew Slifka, who provided additional history about Slifky's and their evolution to Global Partners. Your business has been greatly appreciated.

I want to thank Caroline Myss and my CMED family for keeping me sane over the last twenty-plus years. Working with you, Caroline, has enriched my life as have the people I met through you. Thank you also for helping me define my initial subtitle. You pointed me in the right direction.

Special thanks to Fetneh Eskandari, who read through some of the chapters early on.

Thank you to Dr. Connie Hebert and Kristi Prochazka, who gave me some invaluable feedback as I was writing this book.

Special thanks to my pre-launch team. I appreciate your time!

I am fortunate that I have many friends and family who are dear to me. I appreciate all of your support through the years. Most of all, I appreciate the time spent together. So many good times.

This book was actually started in a cabin in Naples, Maine. Thank you to my Naples family and friends for all of the great times we have shared there.

Mike Koenigs and Ed Rush, your masterminds were incredible. I met some amazing people there too. Ed, I appreciate that you always make time for a phone call. Your support has been invaluable.

Mari Carmen Pizarro, you positively influence so many, including me. Keep up your great work with your company, Whole Leadership Systems, INC., and the Women's Leadership Academy. It is always a pleasure talking to you.

Michael Bernoff, your Human Interaction Technology training was life changing. Thank you for providing many answers.

To Amy Dix of Best Seller Publishing, thank you for all of your book coaching. Matthew Schnarr, thank you for your guidance with all of my editing. And thank you, Rob Kosberg, Bob Harpole, May Cheng, Kathleen Shewman, Lizze Slocum, Meghan McDonald, Liz Huston, and Cole Kosberg for helping me share my ideas with the world! And for working with me to make my book so much better.

In 2019, I was in a car accident where I got a concussion (traumatic brain injury). It was, and still is, a long journey back. It is important when you have a concussion to get the right medical care and not to stop looking for someone to help.

I received my initial help through ATI physical therapy, and then they sent me to an ATI PT who had special training in concussions. I then went to the Cantu Concussion Center for cognitive rehab therapy and vision therapy.

As I still had problems with tinnitus, visual snow, and cognition, I kept looking for doctors to help with those conditions. I found the Mind-Eye Institute in Northbrook, Illinois, near Chicago. The doctors there specialize in neuro-optometric rehabilitation. The eyes are for so much more than seeing.

I had been struggling to write my book. After two years, I was only on Chapter 7. After starting to use their therapeutic eyeglasses and doing their exercises, I was able to finish the rest of the chapters and go through the editing process within a year. I also rewrote some earlier chapters. My point is this: never, ever stop looking for answers. Someone has them.

ABOUT THE AUTHOR

As a Strategic Advisor, *Wall Street Journal* bestselling author Lori Polep helps companies create sustainable businesses that support employees and continual, profitable growth. Her exposure to continuous learning started at a very young age as she listened to her parents discussing challenges and solutions in the businesses they owned. Lori didn't realize it as a child, but those discussions laid a foundation of knowledge for her in a way that many others may never experience.

Lori worked for IBM after earning her Bachelor of Science in Business with a focus in Finance from Boston University. She knew technology was the future. When she returned to her family's business, she was able to create huge opportunities for growth through technological advances. Coupled with her belief in continuous learning, continuous improvement, employee engagement, mentoring, and process improvement, Lori sustained growth, productivity, and efficiency for the company and its employees.

As Vice President and Chief Information Officer, with a Master of Science in Business Management (Communication Technologies) from Rensselaer Polytechnic Institute, Lori is uniquely skilled in problem-solving and process improvement. She saved her company millions of dollars — and through teamwork, sales grew to the tune of $1.3 billion. Additionally, Lori's negotiation expertise continually saved the company money when working with vendors and suppliers.

Lori loves going off the beaten path to find places to explore. She is a Certified Specialist of Wine, so quite often she is visiting vineyards. This is a passion that she enjoys sharing with her friends and family.

www.ingramcontent.com/pod-product-compliance
Lightning Source LLC
Chambersburg PA
CBHW061159120626
46546CB00005B/2117